I0792842

HAGGAI AND MALACHI

WISDOM COMMENTARY

Volume 39

Haggai and Malachi

Stacy Davis

Carol J. Dempsey, OP
Volume Editor

Barbara E. Reid, OP
General Editor

A Michael Glazier Book

LITURGICAL PRESS
Collegeville, Minnesota

www.litpress.org

A Michael Glazier Book published by Liturgical Press

1 2 3 4 5 6 7 8 9

Library of Congress Cataloging-in-Publication Data

Davis, Stacy Nicole.
Haggai and Malachi / Stacy Davis ; Carol Dempsey, volume editor ; Barbara E. Reid, OP, general editor.
pages cm. — (Wisdom commentary ; Volume 39)
"A Michael Glazier book."
Includes bibliographical references and index.
ISBN 978-0-8146-8163-3 — ISBN 978-0-8146-8188-6 (ebook)
1. Bible. Malachi—Commentaries. 2. Bible. Haggai—Commentaries. I. Title.

BS1675.53.D38 2015
224'.97077—dc23 2015018672

For my Hebrew Bible Prophets students,
with gratitude for all that they have taught me
in the last decade,
and for my parents, with love.

Contents

Abbreviations

AB	Anchor Bible
BDB	Brown, Francis, S. R. Driver, and Charles A. Briggs. *A Hebrew and English Lexicon of the Old Testament*
Bib	*Biblica*
BibInt	Biblical Interpretation Series
BN	*Biblische Notizen*
BT	*The Bible Translator*
CBQ	*Catholic Biblical Quarterly*
CurBR	*Currents in Biblical Research*
CurBS	*Currents in Research: Biblical Studies*
CV	*Communio Viatorum*
EstBib	*Estudios bíblicos*
FCB	Feminist Companion to the Bible
HAR	*Hebrew Annual Review*
IFT	Introductions in Feminist Theology
JAAR	*Journal of the American Academy of Religion*
JBL	*Journal of Biblical Literature*
JFSR	*Journal of Feminist Studies in Religion*

JHebS	*Journal of Hebrew Scriptures*
JOTT	*Journal of Translation and Textlinguistics*
JSOT	*Journal for the Study of the Old Testament*
NTS	*New Testament Studies*
NWSA	*National Women's Studies Association*
SBL	Society of Biblical Literature
StBibLit	Studies in Biblical Literature
TynBul	*Tyndale Bulletin*
VT	*Vetus Testamentum*
WTJ	*Westminster Theological Journal*
ZAW	*Zeitschrift für die alttestamentliche Wissenschaft*

Contributors

Rachel Bundang, PhD, is on the theology faculty of the Convent of the Sacred Heart High School in San Francisco.

Rebecca Marie Jones holds a master of arts from the University of Chicago Divinity School.

Rabbi Steven Leapman is a staff therapist at the Samaritan Counseling Center in South Bend, IN.

Carolette Norwood is associate professor of Africana studies and affiliate faculty in women's studies at the University of Cincinnati.

Catherine Punsalan-Manlimos is associate professor of theology and religious studies and director of Catholic studies at Seattle University.

Foreword

"Tell It on the Mountain"—or, "And You Shall Tell Your Daughter [as Well]"

Athalya Brenner-Idan
Universiteit van Amsterdam/Tel Aviv University

What can Wisdom Commentary do to help, and for whom?

The commentary genre has always been privileged in biblical studies. Traditionally acclaimed commentary series, such as the International Critical Commentary, Old Testament and New Testament Library, Hermeneia, Anchor Bible, Eerdmans, and Word—to name but several—enjoy nearly automatic prestige; and the number of women authors who participate in those is relatively small by comparison to their growing number in the scholarly guild. There certainly are some volumes written by women in them, especially in recent decades. At this time, however, this does not reflect the situation on the ground. Further, size matters. In that sense, the sheer size of the Wisdom Commentary is essential. This also represents a considerable investment and the possibility of reaching a wider audience than those already "converted."

Expecting women scholars to deal especially or only with what is considered strictly "female" matters seems unwarranted. According to Audre Lorde, "The master's tools will never dismantle the master's house."[1] But this maxim is not relevant to our case. The point of this commentary is not to destroy but to attain greater participation in the interpretive dialogue about biblical texts. Women scholars may bring additional questions to the readerly agenda as well as fresh angles to existing issues. To assume that their questions are designed only to topple a certain male hegemony is not convincing.

At first I did ask myself: is this commentary series an addition to calm raw nerves, an embellishment to make upholding the old hierarchy palatable? Or is it indeed about becoming the Master? On second and third thoughts, however, I understood that becoming the Master is not what this is about. Knowledge is power. Since Foucault at the very least, this cannot be in dispute. Writing commentaries for biblical texts by women for women and for men, of confessional as well as non-confessional convictions, will sabotage (hopefully) the established hierarchy but will not topple it. This is about an attempt to integrate more fully, to introduce another viewpoint, to become. What excites me about the Wisdom Commentary is that it is not offered as just an alternative supplanting or substituting for the dominant discourse.

These commentaries on biblical books will retain nonauthoritative, pluralistic viewpoints. And yes, once again, the weight of a dedicated series, to distinguish from collections of standalone volumes, will prove weightier.

That such an approach is especially important in the case of the Hebrew Bible/Old Testament is beyond doubt. Women of Judaism, Christianity, and also Islam have struggled to make it their own for centuries, even more than they have fought for the New Testament and the Qur'an. Every Hebrew Bible/Old Testament volume in this project is evidence that the day has arrived: it is now possible to read *all* the Jewish canonical books as a collection, for a collection they are, with guidance conceived of with the needs of women readers (not only men) as an integral inspiration and part thereof.

In my Jewish tradition, the main motivation for reciting the Haggadah, the ritual text recited yearly on Passover, the festival of liberation from

1. Audre Lorde, "The Master's Tools Will Never Dismantle the Master's House," in *Sister Outsider: Essays and Speeches* (Berkeley, CA: Crossing Press, 1984, 2007), 110–14. First delivered in the Second Sex Conference in New York, 1979.

bondage, is given as "And you shall tell your son" (from Exod 13:8). The knowledge and experience of past generations is thus transferred to the next, for constructing the present and the future. The ancient maxim is, literally, limited to a male audience. This series remolds the maxim into a new inclusive shape, which is of the utmost consequence: "And you shall tell your son" is extended to "And you shall tell your daughter [as well as your son]." Or, if you want, "Tell it on the mountain," for all to hear.

This is what it's all about.

Editor's Introduction to Wisdom Commentary

"She Is a Breath of the Power of God" (Wis 7:25)

Barbara E. Reid, OP

General Editor

Wisdom Commentary is the first series to offer detailed feminist interpretation of every book of the Bible. The fruit of collaborative work by an ecumenical and interreligious team of scholars, the volumes provide serious, scholarly engagement with the whole biblical text, not only those texts that explicitly mention women. The series is intended for clergy, teachers, ministers, and all serious students of the Bible. Designed to be both accessible and informed by the various approaches of biblical scholarship, it pays particular attention to the world in front of the text, that is, how the text is heard and appropriated. At the same time, this series aims to be faithful to the ancient text and its earliest audiences; thus the volumes also explicate the worlds behind the text and within it. While issues of gender are primary in this project, the volumes also address the intersecting issues of power, authority, ethnicity, race, class, and religious belief and practice. The fifty-eight volumes include the books regarded as canonical by Jews (i.e., the Tanakh); Protestants (the "Hebrew Bible" and the New Testament); and Roman Catholic, Anglican, and Eastern Orthodox Communions (i.e.,

Tobit, Judith, 1 and 2 Maccabees, Wisdom of Solomon, Sirach/Ecclesiasticus, Baruch, including the Letter of Jeremiah, the additions to Esther, and Susanna and Bel and the Dragon in Daniel).

A Symphony of Diverse Voices

Included in the Wisdom Commentary series are voices from scholars of many different religious traditions, of diverse ages, differing sexual identities, and varying cultural, racial, ethnic, and social contexts. Some have been pioneers in feminist biblical interpretation; others are newer contributors from a younger generation. A further distinctive feature of this series is that each volume incorporates voices other than that of the lead author(s). These voices appear alongside the commentary of the lead author(s) in the grayscale inserts. At times, a contributor may offer an alternative interpretation or a critique of the position taken by the lead author(s). At other times, she or he may offer a complementary interpretation from a different cultural context or subject position. Occasionally, portions of previously published material bring in other views. The diverse voices are not intended to be contestants in a debate or a cacophony of discordant notes. The multiple voices reflect that there is no single definitive feminist interpretation of a text. In addition, they show the importance of subject position in the process of interpretation. In this regard, the Wisdom Commentary series takes inspiration from the Talmud and from *The Torah: A Women's Commentary* (ed. Tamara Cohn Eskenazi and Andrea L. Weiss; New York: Women of Reform Judaism, Federation of Temple Sisterhood, 2008), in which many voices, even conflicting ones, are included and not harmonized.

Contributors include biblical scholars, theologians, and readers of Scripture from outside the scholarly and religious guilds. At times, their comments pertain to a particular text. In some instances they address a theme or topic that arises from the text.

Another feature that highlights the collaborative nature of feminist biblical interpretation is that a number of the volumes have two lead authors who have worked in tandem from the inception of the project and whose voices interweave throughout the commentary.

Woman Wisdom

The title, Wisdom Commentary, reflects both the importance to feminists of the figure of Woman Wisdom in the Scriptures and the distinct wisdom that feminist women and men bring to the interpretive process. In the Scriptures, Woman Wisdom appears as "a breath of the power of God, and a pure emanation of the glory of the Almighty" (Wis 7:25), who was present and active in fashioning all that exists (Prov 8:22-31; Wis 8:6). She is a spirit who pervades and penetrates all things (Wis 7:22-23), and she provides guidance and nourishment at her all-inclusive table (Prov 9:1-5). In both postexilic biblical and nonbiblical Jewish sources, Woman Wisdom is often equated with Torah, e.g., Sir 24:23-34; Bar 3:9–4:4; 38:2; 46:4-5; 2 Bar 48:33, 36; 4 Ezra 5:9-10; 13:55; 14:40; 1 Enoch 42.

The New Testament frequently portrays Jesus as Wisdom incarnate. He invites his followers, "take my yoke upon you and learn from me" (Matt 11:29), just as Ben Sira advises, "put your neck under her [Wisdom's] yoke and let your souls receive instruction" (Sir 51:26). Just as Wisdom experiences rejection (Prov 1:23-25; Sir 15:7-8; Wis 10:3; Bar 3:12), so too does Jesus (Mark 8:31; John 1:10-11). Only some accept his invitation to his all-inclusive banquet (Matt 22:1-14; Luke 14:15-24; compare Prov 1:20-21; 9:3-5). Yet, "wisdom is vindicated by her deeds" (Matt 11:19, speaking of Jesus and John the Baptist; in the Lucan parallel at 7:35 they are called "wisdom's children"). There are numerous parallels between what is said of Wisdom and of the *Logos* in the Prologue of the Fourth Gospel (John 1:1-18). These are only a few of many examples. This female embodiment of divine presence and power is an apt image to guide the work of this series.

Feminism

There are many different understandings of the term "feminism." The various meanings, aims, and methods have developed exponentially in recent decades. Feminism is a perspective and a movement that springs from a recognition of inequities toward women, and it advocates for changes in whatever structures prevent full human flourishing. Three waves of feminism in the United States are commonly recognized. The first, arising in the mid-nineteenth century and lasting into the early twentieth, was sparked by women's efforts to be involved in the public sphere and to win the right to vote. In the 1960s and 1970s, the second wave focused on civil rights and equality for women. With the third wave, from the 1980s forward, came global feminism and the emphasis on the contextual nature of interpretation. As feminism has matured, it has recognized that inequities based on gender are interwoven with power imbalances based on race, class, ethnicity, religion, sexual identity, physical ability, and a host of other social markers.

Feminist Women and Men

Men who choose to identify with and partner with feminist women in the work of deconstructing systems of domination and building structures of equality are rightly regarded as feminists. Some men readily identify with experiences of women who are discriminated against on the basis of sex/gender, having themselves had comparable experiences; others who may not have faced direct discrimination or stereotyping recognize that inequity and problematic characterization still occur, and they seek correction. This series is pleased to include feminist men both as lead authors and as contributing voices.

Feminist Biblical Interpretation

Women interpreting the Bible from the lenses of their own experience is nothing new. Throughout the ages women have recounted the biblical stories, teaching them to their children and others, all the while interpreting them afresh for their time and circumstances.[1] Following is a very brief sketch of select foremothers who laid the groundwork for contemporary feminist biblical interpretation.

One of the earliest known Christian women who challenged patriarchal interpretations of Scripture was a consecrated virgin named Helie, who lived in the second century CE. When she refused to marry, her parents brought her before a judge, who quoted to her Paul's admonition, "It is better to marry than to be aflame with passion" (1 Cor 7:9). In response, Helie first acknowledges that this is what Scripture says, but then she retorts, "but not for everyone, that is, not for holy virgins."[2] She is one of the first to question the notion that a text has one meaning that is applicable in all situations.

A Jewish woman who also lived in the second century CE, Beruriah, is said to have had "profound knowledge of biblical exegesis and out-

1. For fuller treatments of this history, see chap. 7, "One Thousand Years of Feminist Bible Criticism," in Gerda Lerner, *Creation of Feminist Consciousness: From the Middle Ages to Eighteen-Seventy* (New York: Oxford University Press, 1993), 138–66; Susanne Scholz, "From the 'Woman's Bible' to the 'Women's Bible,' The History of Feminist Approaches to the Hebrew Bible," in *Introducing the Women's Hebrew Bible*, IFT 13 (New York: T & T Clark, 2007), 12–32; Marion Ann Taylor and Agnes Choi, eds., *Handbook of Women Biblical Interpreters: A Historical and Biographical Guide* (Grand Rapids, MI: Baker Academic, 2012).

2. Madrid, Escorial MS, a II 9, f. 90 v., as cited in Lerner, *Feminist Consciousness*, 140.

standing intelligence."[3] One story preserved in the Talmud (b. Berachot 10a) tells of how she challenged her husband, Rabbi Meir, when he prayed for the destruction of a sinner. Proffering an alternate interpretation, she argued that Psalm 104:35 advocated praying for the destruction of sin, not the sinner.

In medieval times the first written commentaries on Scripture from a critical feminist point of view emerge. While others may have been produced and passed on orally, they are for the most part lost to us now. Among the earliest preserved feminist writings are those of Hildegard of Bingen (1098–1179), German writer, mystic, and abbess of a Benedictine monastery. She reinterpreted the Genesis narratives in a way that presented women and men as complementary and interdependent. She frequently wrote about feminine aspects of the Divine.[4] Along with other women mystics of the time, such as Julian of Norwich (1342–ca.1416), she spoke authoritatively from her personal experiences of God's revelation in prayer.

In this era, women were also among the scribes who copied biblical manuscripts. Notable among them is Paula Dei Mansi of Verona, from a distinguished family of Jewish scribes. In 1288, she translated from Hebrew into Italian a collection of Bible commentaries written by her father and added her own explanations.[5]

Another pioneer, Christine de Pizan (1365–ca.1430), was a French court writer and prolific poet. She used allegory and common sense to subvert misogynist readings of Scripture and celebrated the accomplishments of female biblical figures to argue for women's active roles in building society.[6]

By the seventeenth century, there were women who asserted that the biblical text needs to be understood and interpreted in its historical context. For example, Rachel Speght (1597–ca.1630), a Calvinist English poet, elaborates on the historical situation in first-century Corinth that prompted Paul to say, "It is well for a man not to touch a woman" (1 Cor

3. See Judith R. Baskin, "Women and Post-Biblical Commentary," in *The Torah: A Women's Commentary*, ed. Tamara Cohn Eskenazi and Andrea L. Weiss (New York: Women of Reform Judaism, Federation of Temple Sisterhood, 2008), xlix–lv, here lii.

4. Hildegard of Bingen, *De Operatione Dei*, 1.4.100; PL 197:885bc, as cited in Lerner, *Feminist Consciousness*, 142–43. See also Barbara Newman, *Sister of Wisdom: St. Hildegard's Theology of the Feminine* (Berkeley: University of California Press, 1987).

5. Emily Taitz, Sondra Henry, Cheryl Tallan, eds., *JPS Guide to Jewish Women 600 B.C.E.–1900 C.E.* (Philadelphia: JPS, 2003), 110–11.

6. See further Taylor and Choi, *Handbook of Women Biblical Interpreters*, 127–32.

7:1). Her aim was to show that the biblical texts should not be applied in a literal fashion to all times and circumstances. Similarly, Margaret Fell (1614–1702), one of the founders of the Religious Society of Friends (Quakers) in Britain, addressed the Pauline prohibitions against women speaking in church by insisting that they do not have universal validity. Rather, they need to be understood in their historical context, as addressed to a local church in particular time-bound circumstances.[7]

Along with analyzing the historical context of the biblical writings, women in the eighteenth and nineteenth centuries began to attend to misogynistic interpretations based on faulty translations. One of the first to do so was British feminist Mary Astell (1666–1731).[8] In the United States, the Grimké sisters, Sarah (1792–1873) and Angelina (1805–1879), Quaker women from a slaveholding family in South Carolina, learned biblical Greek and Hebrew so that they could interpret the Bible for themselves. They were prompted to do so after men sought to silence them from speaking out against slavery and for women's rights by claiming that the Bible (e.g., 1 Cor 14:34) prevented women from speaking in public.[9] Another prominent abolitionist, Sojourner Truth (ca. 1797–1883), a former slave, quoted the Bible liberally in her speeches[10] and in so doing challenged cultural assumptions and biblical interpretations that undergird gender inequities.

Another monumental work that emerged in nineteenth-century England was that of Jewish theologian Grace Aguilar (1816–1847), *The Women of Israel*,[11] published in 1845. Aguilar's approach was to make connections between the biblical women and contemporary Jewish women's concerns. She aimed to counter the widespread notion that women were degraded in Jewish law and that only in Christianity were women's

7. Her major work, *Women's Speaking Justified, Proved and Allowed by the Scriptures*, published in London in 1667, gave a systematic feminist reading of all biblical texts pertaining to women.

8. Mary Astell, *Some Reflections upon Marriage* (New York: Source Book Press, 1970, reprint of the 1730 edition; earliest edition of this work is 1700), 103–4.

9. See further Sarah Grimké, *Letters on the Equality of the Sexes and the Condition of Woman* (Boston: Isaac Knapp, 1838).

10. See, for example, her most famous speech, "Ain't I a Woman?," delivered in 1851 at the Ohio Women's Rights Convention in Akron, OH; http://www.fordham.edu/halsall/mod/sojtruth-woman.asp.

11. The full title is *The Women of Israel or Characters and Sketches from the Holy Scriptures and Jewish History Illustrative of the Past History, Present Duty, and Future Destiny of the Hebrew Females, as Based on the Word of God.*

dignity and value upheld. Her intent was to help Jewish women find strength and encouragement by seeing the evidence of God's compassionate love in the history of every woman in the Bible. While not a full commentary on the Bible, Aguilar's work stands out for its comprehensive treatment of every female biblical character, including even the most obscure references.[12]

The first person to produce a full-blown feminist commentary on the Bible was Elizabeth Cady Stanton (1815–1902). A leading proponent in the United States for women's right to vote, she found that whenever women tried to make inroads into politics, education, or the work world the Bible was quoted against them. Along with a team of like-minded women, she produced her own commentary on every text of the Bible that concerned women. Her pioneering two-volume project, *The Woman's Bible*, published in 1895 and 1898, urges women to recognize that texts that degrade women come from the men who wrote the texts, not from God, and to use their common sense to rethink what has been presented to them as sacred.

Nearly a century later, *The Women's Bible Commentary*, edited by Sharon Ringe and Carol Newsom (Westminster John Knox Press, 1992), appeared. This one-volume commentary features North American feminist scholarship on each book of the Protestant canon. Like Cady Stanton's commentary, it does not contain comments on every section of the biblical text but only on those passages deemed relevant to women. It was revised and expanded in 1998 to include the Apocrypha/Deuterocanonical books, and the contributors to this new volume reflect the global face of contemporary feminist scholarship. The revisions made in the third edition, which appeared in 2012, represent the profound advances in feminist biblical scholarship and include newer voices. In both the second and third editions, *The* has been dropped from the title.

Also appearing at the centennial of Cady Stanton's *The Woman's Bible* were two volumes edited by Elisabeth Schüssler Fiorenza with the assistance of Shelly Matthews. The first, *Searching the Scriptures: A Feminist Introduction* (New York: Crossroad, 1993), charts a comprehensive approach to feminist interpretation from ecumenical, interreligious, and multicultural perspectives. The second volume, published in 1994, provides critical feminist commentary on each book of the New Testament

12. See further Eskenazi and Weiss, *The Torah: A Women's Commentary*, xxxviii; Taylor and Choi, *Handbook of Women Biblical Interpreters*, 31–37.

as well as on three books of Jewish Pseudepigrapha and eleven other early Christian writings.

In Europe, similar endeavors have been undertaken, such as the one-volume *Kompendium Feministische Bibelauslegung*, edited by Luise Schottroff and Marie-Theres Wacker (Gütersloh, Gütersloher Verlagshaus, 2007), featuring German feminist biblical interpretation of each book of the Bible, along with apocryphal books, and several extrabiblical writings. This work, now in its third edition, has recently been translated into English.[13] A multivolume project, *The Bible and Women: An Encylopaedia of Exegesis and Cultural History*, edited by Irmtraud Fischer, Adriana Valerio, Mercedes Navarro Puerto, and Christiana de Groot, is currently in production. This project presents a history of the reception of the Bible as embedded in Western cultural history and focuses particularly on gender-relevant biblical themes, biblical female characters, and women recipients of the Bible. The volumes are published in English, Spanish, Italian, and German.[14]

Another groundbreaking work is the collection The Feminist Companion to the Bible Series, edited by Athalya Brenner (Sheffield: Sheffield Academic Press, 1993–2001). To date, nineteen volumes of commentaries on the Old Testament have been published, with more in production. The parallel series, Feminist Companion to the New Testament and Early Christian Writings, edited by Amy-Jill Levine with Marianne Blickenstaff and Maria Mayo Robbins (Sheffield: Sheffield Academic Press, 2001–2009), contains thirteen volumes with one more planned. These two series are not full commentaries on the biblical books but comprise collected essays on discrete biblical texts.

Works by individual feminist biblical scholars in all parts of the world abound, and they are now too numerous to list in this introduction. Feminist biblical interpretation has reached a level of maturity that now makes possible a commentary series on every book of the Bible. In recent decades, women have had greater access to formal theological education, have been able to learn critical analytical tools, have put their own in-

13. *Feminist Biblical Interpretation: A Compendium of Critical Commentary on the Books of the Bible and Related Literature*, trans. Lisa E. Dahill, Everett R. Kalin, Nancy Lukens, Linda M. Maloney, Barbara Rumscheidt, Martin Rumscheidt, and Tina Steiner (Grand Rapids, MI: Eerdmans, 2012).

14. The first volume, on the Torah, appeared in Spanish in 2009, in German and Italian in 2010, and in English in 2011 (Atlanta, GA: SBL). For further information, see http://www.bibleandwomen.org.

terpretations into writing, and have developed new methods of biblical interpretation. Until recent decades, the work of feminist biblical interpreters was largely unknown, both to other women and to their brothers in the synagogue, church, and academy. Feminists now have taken their place in the professional world of biblical scholars, where they build on the work of their foremothers and connect with one another across the globe in ways not previously possible. In a few short decades, feminist biblical criticism has become an integral part of the academy.

Methodologies

Feminist biblical scholars use a variety of methods and often employ a number of them together.[15] In the Wisdom Commentary series, the authors will explain their understanding of feminism and the feminist reading strategies used in their commentary. Each volume treats the biblical text in blocks of material, not an analysis verse by verse. The entire text is considered, not only those passages that feature female characters or that speak specifically about women. When women are not apparent in the narrative, feminist lenses are used to analyze the dynamics in the text between male characters, the models of power, binary ways of thinking, and dynamics of imperialism. Attention is given to how the whole text functions and how it was and is heard, both in its original context and today. Issues of particular concern to women—e.g., poverty, food, health, the environment, water—come to the fore.

One of the approaches used by early feminists and still popular today is to lift up the overlooked and forgotten stories of women in the Bible. Studies of women in each of the Testaments have been done, and there are also studies on women in particular biblical books.[16] Feminists recognize that the examples of biblical characters can be both

15. See the seventeen essays in Caroline Vander Stichele and Todd Penner, eds., *Her Master's Tools? Feminist and Postcolonial Engagements of Historical-Critical Discourse* (Atlanta, GA: SBL, 2005), which show the complementarity of various approaches.

16. See, e.g., Alice Bach, ed., *Women in the Hebrew Bible: A Reader* (New York: Routledge, 1998); Tikva Frymer-Kensky, *Reading the Women of the Bible* (New York: Schocken, 2002); Carol Meyers, Toni Craven, and Ross S. Kraemer, *Women in Scripture* (Grand Rapids, MI: Eerdmans, 2000); Irene Nowell, *Women in the Old Testament* (Collegeville, MN: Liturgical Press, 1997); Katharine Doob Sakenfeld, *Just Wives? Stories of Power and Survival in the Old Testament and Today* (Louisville, KY: Westminster John Knox, 2003);

empowering and problematic. The point of the feminist enterprise is not to serve as an apologetic for women; it is rather, in part, to recover women's history and literary roles in all their complexity and to learn from that recovery.

Retrieving the submerged history of biblical women is a crucial step for constructing the story of the past so as to lead to liberative possibilities for the present and future. There are, however, some pitfalls to this approach. Sometimes depictions of biblical women have been naïve and romantic. Some commentators exalt the virtues of both biblical and contemporary women and paint women as superior to men. Such reverse discrimination inhibits movement toward equality for all. In addition, some feminists challenge the idea that one can "pluck positive images out of an admittedly androcentric text, separating literary characterizations from the androcentric interests they were created to serve."[17] Still other feminists find these images to have enormous value.

One other danger with seeking the submerged history of women is the tendency for Christian feminists to paint Jesus and even Paul as liberators of women in a way that demonizes Judaism.[18] Wisdom Commentary aims to enhance understanding of Jesus as well as Paul as Jews of their day and to forge solidarity among Jewish and Christian feminists.

Feminist scholars who use historical-critical methods analyze the world behind the text; they seek to understand the historical context from which the text emerged and the circumstances of the communities to whom it was addressed. In bringing feminist lenses to this approach, the aim is not to impose modern expectations on ancient cultures but to unmask the ways that ideologically problematic mind-sets that produced the ancient texts are still promulgated through the text. Feminist biblical scholars aim not only to deconstruct but also to reclaim and reconstruct biblical history as women's history, in which women were central and

---

Mary Ann Getty-Sullivan, *Women in the New Testament* (Collegeville, MN: Liturgical Press, 2001); Bonnie Thurston, *Women in the New Testament* (New York: Crossroad, 1998).

17. Cheryl Exum, "Second Thoughts about Secondary Characters: Women in Exodus 1.8–2.10," in *A Feminist Companion to Exodus to Deuteronomy*, FCB 6 (Sheffield: Sheffield Academic Press, 1994), 75–97, here 76.

18. See Judith Plaskow, "Anti-Judaism in Feminist Christian Interpretation," in *Searching the Scriptures: A Feminist Introduction* (New York: Crossroad, 1993), 1:117–29; Amy-Jill Levine, "The New Testament and Anti-Judaism," in *The Misunderstood Jew: The Church and the Scandal of the Jewish Jesus* (San Francisco: HarperSanFrancisco, 2006), 87–117.

active agents in creating religious heritage.[19] A further step is to construct meaning for contemporary women and men in a liberative movement toward transformation of social, political, economic, and religious structures.[20] In recent years, some feminists have embraced new historicism, which accents the creative role of the interpreter in any construction of history and exposes the power struggles to which the text witnesses.[21]

Literary critics analyze the world of the text: its form, language patterns, and rhetorical function.[22] They do not attempt to separate layers of tradition and redaction but focus on the text holistically, as it is in its present form. They examine how meaning is created in the interaction between the text and its reader in multiple contexts. Within the arena of literary approaches are reader-oriented approaches, narrative, rhetorical, structuralist, post-structuralist, deconstructive, ideological, autobiographical, and performance criticism.[23] Narrative critics study the

19. See, for example, Phyllis A. Bird, *Missing Persons and Mistaken Identities: Women and Gender in Ancient Israel* (Minneapolis: Fortress Press, 1997); Elisabeth Schüssler Fiorenza, *In Memory of Her: A Feminist Theological Reconstruction of Christian Origins* (New York: Crossroad, 1984); Ross Shepard Kraemer and Mary Rose D'Angelo, eds., *Women and Christian Origins* (New York: Oxford University Press, 1999).

20. See, e.g., Sandra M. Schneiders, *The Revelatory Text: Interpreting the New Testament as Sacred Scripture*, rev. ed. (Collegeville, MN: Liturgical Press, 1999), whose aim is to engage in biblical interpretation not only for intellectual enlightenment but, even more important, for personal and communal transformation. Elisabeth Schüssler Fiorenza (*Wisdom Ways: Introducing Feminist Biblical Interpretation* [Maryknoll, NY: Orbis Books, 2001]) envisions the work of feminist biblical interpretation as a dance of Wisdom that consists of seven steps that interweave in spiral movements toward liberation, the final one being transformative action for change.

21. See Gina Hens Piazza, *The New Historicism*, Guides to Biblical Scholarship, Old Testament Series (Minneapolis: Fortress Press, 2002).

22. Phyllis Trible was among the first to employ this method with texts from Genesis and Ruth in her groundbreaking book *God and the Rhetoric of Sexuality*, Overtures to Biblical Theology (Philadelphia: Fortress Press, 1978). Another pioneer in feminist literary criticism is Mieke Bal (*Lethal Love: Feminist Literary Readings of Biblical Love Stories* [Bloomington: Indiana University Press, 1987]). For surveys of recent developments in literary methods, see Terry Eagleton, *Literary Theory: An Introduction*, 3rd ed. (Minneapolis: University of Minnesota Press, 2008); Janice Capel Anderson and Stephen D. Moore, eds., *Mark and Method: New Approaches in Biblical Studies*, 2nd ed. (Minneapolis: Fortress Press, 2008).

23. See, e.g., J. Cheryl Exum and David J. A. Clines, eds., *The New Literary Criticism and the Hebrew Bible* (Valley Forge, PA: Trinity Press International, 1993); Edgar V. McKnight and Elizabeth Struthers Malbon, eds., *The New Literary Criticism and the New Testament* (Valley Forge, PA: Trinity Press International, 1994).

interrelation among author, text, and audience through investigation of settings, both spatial and temporal; characters; plot; and narrative techniques (e.g., irony, parody, intertextual allusions). Reader-response critics attend to the impact that the text has on the reader or hearer. They recognize that when a text is detrimental toward women there is the choice either to affirm the text or to read against the grain toward a liberative end. Rhetorical criticism analyzes the style of argumentation and attends to how the author is attempting to shape the thinking or actions of the hearer. Structuralist critics analyze the complex patterns of binary oppositions in the text to derive its meaning.[24] Post-structuralist approaches challenge the notion that there are fixed meanings to any biblical text or that there is one universal truth. They engage in close readings of the text and often engage in intertextual analysis.[25] Within this approach is deconstructionist criticism, which views the text as a site of conflict, with competing narratives. The interpreter aims to expose the fault lines and overturn and reconfigure binaries by elevating the underling of a pair and foregrounding it.[26] Feminists also use other postmodern approaches, such as ideological and autobiographical criticism. The former analyzes the system of ideas that underlies the power and values concealed in the text as well as that of the interpreter.[27] The latter involves deliberate self-disclosure while reading the text as a critical exegete.[28] Performance criticism attends to how the text was passed on orally, usually in com-

24. See, e.g., David Jobling, *The Sense of Biblical Narrative: Three Structural Analyses in the Old Testament*, JSOTSup 7 (Sheffield: Sheffield University, 1978).

25. See, e.g., Stephen D. Moore, *Poststructuralism and the New Testament: Derrida and Foucault at the Foot of the Cross* (Minneapolis: Fortress Press, 1994); *The Bible in Theory: Critical and Postcritical Essays* (Atlanta, GA: SBL, 2010); Yvonne Sherwood, *A Biblical Text and Its Afterlives: The Survival of Jonah in Western Culture* (Cambridge: Cambridge University Press, 2000).

26. David Penchansky, "Deconstruction," in *The Oxford Encyclopedia of Biblical Interpretation*, ed. Steven McKenzie (New York: Oxford University Press, 2013), 196–205. See, for example, Danna Nolan Fewell and David M. Gunn, *Gender, Power, and Promise: The Subject of the Bible's First Story* (Nashville, TN: Abingdon, 1993); David Rutledge, *Reading Marginally: Feminism, Deconstruction and the Bible*, BibInt 21 (Leiden: Brill, 1996).

27. See Tina Pippin, ed., *Ideological Criticism of Biblical Texts: Semeia* 59 (1992); Terry Eagleton, *Ideology: An Introduction* (London: Verso, 2007).

28. See, e.g., Ingrid Rose Kitzberger, ed., *Autobiographical Biblical Interpretation: Between Text and Self* (Leiden: Deo, 2002); P. J. W. Schutte, "When *They*, *We*, and the Passive Become *I*—Introducing Autobiographical Biblical Criticism," *HTS Teologiese Studies / Theological Studies* 61 (2005): 401–16.

munal settings, and to the verbal and nonverbal interactions between the performer and the audience.[29]

From the beginning, feminists have understood that interpreting the Bible is an act of power. In recent decades, feminist biblical scholars have developed hermeneutical theories of the ethics and politics of biblical interpretation to challenge the claims to value neutrality of most academic biblical scholarship. Feminist biblical scholars have also turned their attention to how some biblical writings were shaped by the power of empire and how this still shapes readers' self-understandings today. They have developed hermeneutical approaches that reveal, critique, and evaluate the interactions depicted in the text against the context of empire, and they consider implications for contemporary contexts.[30] Feminists also analyze the dynamics of colonization and the mentalities of colonized peoples in the exercise of biblical interpretation. As Kwok Pui-lan explains, "A postcolonial feminist interpretation of the Bible needs to investigate the deployment of gender in the narration of identity, the negotiation of power differentials between the colonizers and the colonized, and the reinforcement of patriarchal control over spheres where these elites could exercise control."[31] Methods and models from sociology and cultural anthropology are used by feminists to investigate women's everyday lives, their experiences of marriage, childrearing, labor, money, illness, etc.[32]

29. See, e.g., Holly Hearon and Philip Ruge-Jones, eds., *The Bible in Ancient and Modern Media: Story and Performance* (Eugene, OR: Cascade Books, 2009).

30. E.g., Gale Yee, ed., *Judges and Method: New Approaches in Biblical Studies* (Minneapolis: Fortress Press, 1995); Warren Carter, *The Gospel of Matthew in Its Roman Imperial Context* (London: T & T Clark, 2005); *The Roman Empire and the New Testament: An Essential Guide* (Nashville, TN: Abingdon, 2006); Elisabeth Schüssler Fiorenza, *The Power of the Word: Scripture and the Rhetoric of Empire* (Minneapolis: Fortress, 2007); Judith E. McKinlay, *Reframing Her: Biblical Women in Postcolonial Focus* (Sheffield: Sheffield Phoenix Press, 2004).

31. Kwok Pui-lan, *Postcolonial Imagination and Feminist Theology* (Louisville, KY: Westminster John Knox, 2005), 9. See also Musa W. Dube, ed., *Postcolonial Feminist Interpretation of the Bible* (St. Louis, MO: Chalice, 2000); Cristl M. Maier and Carolyn J. Sharp, *Prophecy and Power: Jeremiah in Feminist and Postcolonial Perspective* (London: Bloomsbury, 2013).

32. See, for example, Carol Meyers, *Discovering Eve: Ancient Israelite Women in Context* (New York: Oxford University Press, 1991); Luise Schottroff, *Lydia's Impatient Sisters: A Feminist Social History of Early Christianity*, trans. Barbara and Martin Rumscheidt (Louisville, KY: Westminster John Knox, 1995); Susan Niditch, *"My Brother Esau Is a Hairy Man": Hair and Identity in Ancient Israel* (Oxford: Oxford University Press, 2008).

As feminists have examined the construction of gender from varying cultural perspectives, they have become ever more cognizant that the way gender roles are defined within differing cultures varies radically. As Mary Ann Tolbert observes, "Attempts to isolate some universal role that cross-culturally defines 'woman' have run into contradictory evidence at every turn."[33] Some women have coined new terms to highlight the particularities of their socio-cultural context. Many African American feminists, for example, call themselves *womanists* to draw attention to the double oppression of racism and sexism they experience.[34] Similarly, many U.S. Hispanic feminists speak of themselves as *mujeristas* (*mujer* is Spanish for "woman").[35] Others prefer to be called "Latina feminists."[36] Both groups emphasize that the context for their theologizing is *mestizaje* and *mulatez* (racial and cultural mixture), done *en conjunto* (in community), with *lo cotidiano* (everyday lived experience) of Hispanic women as starting points for theological reflection and the encounter with the divine. Intercultural analysis has become an indispensable tool for working toward justice for women at the global level.[37]

Some feminists are among those who have developed lesbian, gay, bisexual, and transgender (LGBT) interpretation. This approach focuses on issues of sexual identity and uses various reading strategies. Some point out the ways in which categories that emerged in recent centuries are applied anachronistically to biblical texts to make modern-day judgments. Others show how the Bible is silent on contemporary issues about

33. Mary Ann Tolbert, "Social, Sociological, and Anthropological Methods," in *Searching the Scriptures*, 1:255–71, here 265.

34. Alice Walker coined the term (*In Search of Our Mothers' Gardens: Womanist Prose* [New York: Harcourt Brace Jovanovich, 1967, 1983]). See also Katie G. Cannon, "The Emergence of Black Feminist Consciousness," in *Feminist Interpretation of the Bible*, ed. Letty M. Russell (Philadelphia: Westminster, 1985), 30–40; Nyasha Junior, "Womanist Biblical Interpretation," in *Engaging the Bible in a Gendered World: An Introduction to Feminist Biblical Interpretation in Honor of Katharine Doob Sakenfeld*, ed. Linda Day and Carolyn Pressler (Louisville, KY: Westminster John Knox, 2006), 37–46; Renita Weems, *Just a Sister Away: A Womanist Vision of Women's Relationships in the Bible* (San Diego: Lura Media, 1988).

35. Ada María Isasi-Díaz (*Mujerista Theology: A Theology for the Twenty-first Century* [Maryknoll, NY: Orbis Books, 1996]) is credited with coining the term.

36. E.g., María Pilar Aquino, Daisy L. Machado, and Jeanette Rodríguez, eds., *A Reader in Latina Feminist Theology* (Austin: University of Texas Press, 2002).

37. See, e.g., María Pilar Aquino and María José Rosado-Nunes, eds., *Feminist Intercultural Theology: Latina Explorations for a Just World*, Studies in Latino/a Catholicism (Maryknoll, NY: Orbis Books, 2007).

sexual identity. Still others examine same-sex relationships in the Bible by figures such as Ruth and Naomi or David and Jonathan. In recent years, queer theory has emerged; it emphasizes the blurriness of boundaries not just of sexual identity but also of gender roles. Queer critics often focus on texts in which figures transgress what is traditionally considered proper gender behavior.[38]

Feminists also recognize that the struggle for women's equality and dignity is intimately connected with the struggle for respect for Earth and for the whole of the cosmos. Ecofeminists interpret Scripture in ways that highlight the link between human domination of nature and male subjugation of women. They show how anthropocentric ways of interpreting the Bible have overlooked or dismissed Earth and Earth community. They invite readers to identify not only with human characters in the biblical narrative but also with other Earth creatures and domains of nature, especially those that are the object of injustice. Some use creative imagination to retrieve the interests of Earth implicit in the narrative and enable Earth to speak.[39]

Biblical Authority

By the late nineteenth century, some feminists, such as Elizabeth Cady Stanton, began to question openly whether the Bible could continue to be regarded as authoritative for women. They viewed the Bible itself as the source of women's oppression, and some rejected its sacred origin and saving claims. Some decided that the Bible and the religious traditions that enshrine it are too thoroughly saturated with androcentrism and patriarchy to be redeemable.[40]

38. See, e.g., Bernadette J. Brooten, *Love between Women: Early Christian Responses to Female Homoeroticism* (Chicago and London: University of Chicago Press, 1996); Mary Rose D'Angelo, "Women Partners in the New Testament," *JFSR* 6 (1990): 65–86; Deirdre J. Good, "Reading Strategies for Biblical Passages on Same-Sex Relations," *Theology and Sexuality* 7 (1997): 70–82; Deryn Guest, *When Deborah Met Jael: Lesbian Feminist Hermeneutics* (London: SCM, 2011); Teresa Hornsby and Ken Stone, eds., *Bible Trouble: Queer Readings at the Boundaries of Biblical Scholarship* (Atlanta, GA: SBL, 2011).

39. E.g., Norman C. Habel and Peter Trudinger, *Exploring Ecological Hermeneutics*, SBLSymS 46 (Atlanta, GA: SBL, 2008); Mary Judith Ress, *Ecofeminism in Latin America*, Women from the Margins (Maryknoll, NY: Orbis Books, 2006).

40. E.g., Mary Daly, *Beyond God the Father: A Philosophy of Women's Liberation* (London: The Women's Press, 1986).

In the Wisdom Commentary series, questions such as these may be raised, but the aim of this series is not to lead readers to reject the authority of the biblical text. Rather, the aim is to promote better understanding of the contexts from which the text arose and of the rhetorical effects it has on women and men in contemporary contexts. Such understanding can lead to a deepening of faith, with the Bible serving as an aid to bring flourishing of life.

Language for God

Because of the ways in which the term "God" has been used to symbolize the divine in predominantly male, patriarchal, and monarchical modes, feminists have designed new ways of speaking of the divine. Some have called attention to the inadequacy of the term *God* by trying to visually destabilize our ways of thinking and speaking of the divine. Rosemary Radford Ruether proposed *God/ess*, as an unpronounceable term pointing to the unnameable understanding of the divine that transcends patriarchal limitations.[41] Some have followed traditional Jewish practice, writing *G-d*. Elisabeth Schüssler Fiorenza has adopted *G*d*.[42] Others draw on the biblical tradition to mine female and non-gender-specific metaphors and symbols.[43] In Wisdom Commentary, there is not one standard way of expressing the divine; each author will use her or his preferred ways. The one exception is that when the tetragrammaton, YHWH, the name revealed to Moses in Exodus 3:14, is used, it will be without vowels, respecting the Jewish custom of avoiding pronouncing the divine name out of reverence.

Nomenclature for the Two Testaments

In recent decades, some biblical scholars have begun to call the two Testaments of the Bible by names other than the traditional nomencla-

41. Rosemary Radford Ruether, *Sexism and God-Talk: Toward a Feminist Theology* (Boston: Beacon, 1983).

42. Elisabeth Schüssler Fiorenza, *Jesus: Miriam's Child, Sophia's Prophet; Critical Issues in Feminist Christology* (New York: Continuum, 1994), 191 n. 3.

43. E.g., Sallie McFague, *Models of God: Theology for an Ecological, Nuclear Age* (Philadelphia: Fortress Press, 1987); Catherine LaCugna, *God for Us: The Trinity and Christian Life* (San Francisco: Harper Collins, 1991); Elizabeth A. Johnson, *She Who Is: The Mystery of God in Feminist Theological Discourse* (New York: Crossroad, 1992). See further Elizabeth A. Johnson, "God," in *Dictionary of Feminist Theologies*, 128–30.

ture: Old and New Testament. Some regard "Old" as derogatory, implying that it is no longer relevant or that it has been superseded. Consequently, terms like Hebrew Bible, First Testament, and Jewish Scriptures and, correspondingly, Christian Scriptures or Second Testament have come into use. There are a number of difficulties with these designations. The term "Hebrew Bible" does not take into account that parts of the Old Testament are written not in Hebrew but in Aramaic.[44] Moreover, for Roman Catholics, Anglicans, and Eastern Orthodox believers, the Old Testament includes books written in Greek—the Deuterocanonical books, considered Apocrypha by Protestants. The term "Jewish Scriptures" is inadequate because these books are also sacred to Christians. Conversely, "Christian Scriptures" is not an accurate designation for the New Testament, since the Old Testament is also part of the Christian Scriptures. Using "First and Second Testament" also has difficulties, in that it can imply a hierarchy and a value judgment.[45] Jews generally use the term Tanakh, an acronym for Torah (Pentateuch), Nevi'im (Prophets), and Ketuvim (Writings).

In Wisdom Commentary, if authors choose to use a designation other than Tanakh, Old Testament, and New Testament, they will explain how they mean the term.

Translation

Modern feminist scholars recognize the complexities connected with biblical translation, as they have delved into questions about philosophy of language, how meanings are produced, and how they are culturally situated. Today it is evident that simply translating into gender-neutral formulations cannot address all the challenges presented by androcentric texts. Efforts at feminist translation must also deal with issues around authority and canonicity.[46]

Because of these complexities, the editors of Wisdom Commentary series have chosen to use an existing translation, the New Revised Standard Version (NRSV), which is provided for easy reference at the top of each page of commentary. The NRSV was produced by a team of ecumenical and interreligious scholars, is a fairly literal translation, and uses

44. Gen 31:47; Jer 10:11; Ezra 4:7–6:18; 7:12-26; Dan 2:4–7:28.

45. See Levine, *The Misunderstood Jew*, 193–99.

46. Elizabeth Castelli, "*Les Belles Infidèles*/Fidelity or Feminism? The Meanings of Feminist Biblical Translation," in *Searching the Scriptures*, 1:189–204, here 190.

inclusive language for human beings. Brief discussions about problematic translations appear in the inserts labeled "Translation Matters." When more detailed discussions are available, these will be indicated in footnotes. In the commentary, wherever Hebrew or Greek words are used, English translation is provided. In cases where a wordplay is involved, transliteration is provided to enable understanding.

Art and Poetry

Artistic expression in poetry, music, sculpture, painting, and various other modes is very important to feminist interpretation. Where possible, art and poetry is included in the print volumes of the series. In a number of instances, these are original works created for this project. Regrettably, copyright and production costs prohibit the inclusion of color photographs and other artistic work. It is our hope that the web version will allow a greater collection of such resources.

Glossary

Because there are a number of excellent readily-available resources that provide definitions and concise explanations of terms used in feminist theological and biblical studies, this series will not include a glossary. We refer you to works such as *Dictionary of Feminist Theologies*, edited by Letty M. Russell with J. Shannon Clarkson (Louisville: Westminster John Knox, 1996), and volume 1 of *Searching the Scriptures*, edited by Elisabeth Schüssler Fiorenza with the assistance of Shelly Matthews (New York: Crossroad, 1992). Individual authors in the Wisdom Commentary series will define the way they are using terms that may be unfamiliar.

Bibliography

Because bibliographies are quickly outdated and because the space is limited, only a list of Works Cited is included in the print volumes. A comprehensive bibliography for each volume is posted on a dedicated website and is updated regularly.

The link for this volume is: wisdomcommentary.org.

A Concluding Word

In just a few short decades, feminist biblical studies has grown exponentially, both in the methods that have been developed and in the num-

The books have different structures but share a common theological problem: how to persuade the people to obey divine imperatives. Interestingly, Mark J. Boda notes that Haggai and Malachi have the highest ratio of messenger formulae (e.g., "says YHWH") in the prophetic canon.[3] Comparing these two prophets to Amos, fourth on the list of messenger formulae, Boda concludes that increased appearances of the phrase suggest a problem with "the authority and authenticity of his prophetic words"; the heavy presence of messenger formulae in Haggai and Malachi "may be a window into a sceptical attitude of the Persian community towards prophecy that may have been fostered by the late pre-exilic crisis in the prophetic movement."[4] Both Haggai and Malachi assume the validity of the theory of divine retribution in which God rewards the righteous and punishes the wicked, but even with that assumption, each book portrays God as a parent struggling to maintain or regain control over rebelliously apathetic children. Haggai's God promises future blessings, while Malachi's God resorts to threats. The difference between the two may come from the historical context of the biblical texts.

Both books lend themselves to diachronic and well as synchronic interpretations. As a rhetorical critic, methodologically I have chosen at times to focus solely on the text (synchronic) and at other times to include such things as names, dates, and times (diachronic).[5] The fact that the prophet Haggai wants to persuade a community one generation removed from a crisis-inducing exile shapes his language, which chastises the returned exiles, but speaks even more harshly against the nations (Hag 2:6-7, 21-22). In contrast, Malachi's railing against his community comes generations after the exile, when perhaps less justification remains for the people's bad behavior; life, by now, should be "back to normal," and the temple should receive the respect and offerings that are its due. How each community responds to the prophet depends on both historical context and subject location.

Context and location are needed, since by itself, the phrase "subject location" may be limiting from a feminist theoretical perspective. In a 2005 essay for the *NWSA Journal*, Aimee Carrillo Rowe argues for a

3. Mark J. Boda, "Haggai: Master Rhetorician," *TynBul* 51 (2000): 298.

4. Ibid., 299.

5. Patricia K. Tull, "Rhetorical Criticism and Intertextuality," in *To Each Its Own Meaning: An Introduction to Biblical Criticisms and Their Applications*, ed. Steven L. McKenzie and Stephen R. Haynes, rev. and exp. ed. (Louisville, KY: Westminster John Knox, 1999), 159.

feminist rethinking of subject location. Rowe suggests that focusing on the subject limits the interconnections all subjects have with other people and communities.[6] While writing specifically about the feminist turn to the subject, Rowe's words apply to Haggai and Malachi as well: "What often gets overlooked in the framework of 'identity' (or 'location' as above) are the ways in which dominant identity categories interpellate subjects through regulatory practices that essentially condition belonging."[7] In other words, while both prophets (and particularly Malachi) use specific identity markers to describe their interlocutors, those markers attempt to limit the ways that the people in both books should be understood. The categories function as rhetorical weapons; the prophets want the reader/listener to see the people as *they* do. If, however, "one of the tasks of feminist criticism is to expose the culturally based presuppositions embodied in classic discourse,"[8] then resisting the prophets' identification of the people as "subjects," specifically disobedient worshipers, and thinking about how the people in that postexilic time and place may have viewed their world is a useful feminist exercise.

Haggai and Malachi lend themselves to feminist analysis because of the intersectionality of gender, class, and religion with relationships of power and authority. Underneath the two books runs a strong and often nasty undercurrent of power—who has it, who does not, and who wants it? Danna Nolan Fewell notes in her definitions of feminist criticism that "gender is a matter of power. . . . Men have power over women socially, politically, and economically. Race and class further complicate the hierarchy of dominance. Such hierarchy is inscribed in our classic texts, presupposed as if it were natural law rather than cultural construct."[9] In her New Testament scholarship, Elisabeth Schüssler Fiorenza describes intersectionality as the "multiplicative structures of oppression . . . that determine and diminish all of our lives."[10] Haggai and Malachi both describe a hierarchy in which God, through designated male representa-

6. Aimee Carrillo Rowe, "Be Longing: Toward a Feminist Politics of Relation," *NWSA Journal* 17 (2005): 16.

7. Ibid., 28.

8. Danna Nolan Fewell, "Feminist Criticism," in *To Each Its Own Meaning: An Introduction to Biblical Criticisms and Their Applications*, ed. Steven L. McKenzie and Stephen R. Haynes, rev. and exp. ed. (Louisville, KY: Westminster John Knox, 1999), 270.

9. Ibid., 269–70.

10. Elisabeth Schüssler Fiorenza, *Jesus: Miriam's Child, Sophia's Prophet: Critical Issues in Feminist Christology* (New York: Continuum, 1994), 12, 13.

tives, exercises power over other men. The priests and prophets speak; the masses should obey.

Because of the tendency to view hierarchy as all men above all women, without always considering that not all men are equal, Schüssler Fiorenza's definition of kyriarchy offers a helpful feminist theoretical foundation for readings of Haggai and Malachi. Schüssler Fiorenza writes as follows: "I have argued for a redefinition of the concept of patriarchy to mean not simply the rule of men over women but rather a complex social pyramid of graduated dominations and subordinations. Because feminist discourses continue to use the term 'patriarchy' in the sense of gender dualism, I introduced in *But She Said* the neologism 'kyriarchy,' meaning the rule of the emperor/master/lord/father/husband over his subordinates. With this term I mean to indicate that not all men dominate and exploit all women without difference."[11] Unlike "patriarchy," "kyriarchy" reveals that men can and do dominate other men in particular contexts, which is precisely what we hear in Haggai and especially Malachi.

Instead of patriarchy or kyriarchy, Carol L. Meyers argues persuasively for the use of "heterarchy" to describe the idea of different power arrangements within a society, recognizing that such arrangements need not always be vertical ones. She writes: "Perhaps [heterarchy's] most attractive feature is that it does not eliminate hierarchies but rather recognizes that there can be a variety of heterarchies that may or may not intersect with each other. That is, heterarchies and hierarchies are not mutually exclusive concepts but rather interactive or dialectical ones."[12] As father and master in Malachi, God demands obedience from his sons and slaves. They never grow up and become the father. And yet, they are men, who argue with each other about how to behave (or not). Heterarchy reveals—and my commentary explores—the tension between the expected obedience of earthly men to the divine "man," which the prophets articulate, as well as the resistance to that expectation.

Precisely because of the questions Haggai and Malachi raise about masculinity, masculine language and male pronouns for God appear intentionally in this commentary. Most contributors to this series will not use male-dominant language, and I understand and usually agree with this, regularly avoiding any pronouns for God in my scholarship. In this case, however, I make an exception. Since I argue that both books

11. Ibid., 14.

12. Carol L. Meyers, *Rediscovering Eve: Ancient Israelite Women in Context* (Oxford: Oxford University Press, 2013), 197.

describe a crisis between a personified male God and his male followers, the pronouns matter and should be heard in their original linguistic context. Hebrew has no neuter, as Rebecca Marie Jones (one of this volume's contributing voices) learned in her research about gendered language in Reform Jewish prayer books. While gender-neutral language for God may sound "better" in English, the Hebrew language and imagery for God remain masculine, whether one says the male pronouns or not. From a rhetorical perspective, language matters; hearing the pronouns will hopefully draw the reader into the ancient masculine drama that Haggai and Malachi describe.

The God described in Haggai's and Malachi's attempts to assert divine authority may also be explained using the language of masculinity studies as well as feminist theory. Historical studies indicate "that definitions of masculinity are deeply enmeshed in the history of institutions and of economic structures. Masculinity is not just an idea in the head, or a personal identity. It is also extended in the world, merged in organized social relations."[13] In the social world of Haggai and Malachi, "authentic men" worship God and support the hierarchical temple structure, reestablishing the building and bringing a steady supply of offerings. This priestly oriented identity acts as a type of hegemonic masculinity, or the dominant masculine ideal in a particular cultural or social context.[14] As Raewyn W. Connell notes, "'Hegemonic masculinity' is not a fixed character type, always and everywhere the same. It is, rather, the masculinity that occupies the hegemonic position in a given pattern of gender relations, a position always contestable."[15] Haggai's call to rebuild the temple reinforces the position of the priests; as recipients of the sacrifices, the restoration of the temple literally restores their livelihood. They and their political and religious supporters eventually persuade the people to heed the rebuilding call, and "it is the successful claim to authority, more than direct violence, that is the mark of hegemony."[16]

A challenge to the priests' masculine hegemony, however, comes in Malachi. The sacrifices decrease in quality (Mal 1:6-14) and quantity (Mal 3:8-12), and even the priests themselves appear to reject their own authority by accepting the new state of sacrificial affairs (Mal 2:1-9). The

13. Raewyn W. Connell, *Masculinities*, 2nd ed. (Berkeley: University of California Press, 2005), 29.

14. Ibid., 37.

15. Ibid., 76.

16. Ibid., 77.

connection between masculinity and power, an "insight . . . of Fundamental importance,"[17] has broken down, and the prophet's attempts to reinforce tradition meet with sustained resistance from the people. Connell argues that men "who reject the hegemonic pattern have to fight or negotiate their way out."[18] In the case of Malachi, the men neither fight nor negotiate; they simply refuse to play along.

But why stop playing? In Hag 1, the people's reluctance to stop everything else and rebuild the temple may be due to the importance of everything else—rebuilding ruined homes left vacant from the exile, reestablishing fields and vineyards, and restoring flocks and herds. Malachi's context is more elusive. The prophet suggests in Mal 1 that the people have the resources and simply will not contribute to the temple. Therefore, the people are greedy. The chapter, however, suggests that the people believe the sacrificial system no longer works: if offerings to God do not bring the expected rewards, why bother making offerings at all? Therefore, the people are in theological crisis. Since they do not get to speak for themselves, we may never know whether they were greedy, destitute, both, or neither. Malachi's emphasis on animal sacrifices, however, presumes an audience not stricken by poverty because the poor did not have to sacrifice animals that they neither had nor could afford (Lev 5:11-13).

Practically, the refusal to play along triggers social consequences. According to Num 18, the priests and Levites deliberately receive no land; as full-time servants of God, their duties keep them from agricultural tasks. Instead, they receive tithes and offerings from the other Israelites, of grain, wine, oil, and meat. If those offerings diminish, then the food source for the priests and their families diminishes as well. Malachi's protest about sacrifices and tithing and insistence upon their restoration serves more than a religious purpose. By arguing for the continuation of the existing structure of protein exchange (the people give food to the priests), the prophet describes what anthropologists call resource flow, or how goods and services move from one group or community to

17. Ibid., 42.

18. Ibid., 37. Similarly, gender studies scholar Todd W. Reeser (*Masculinities in Theory: An Introduction* [West Sussex, UK: Wiley-Blackwell, 2010], 34) states that "no discursive construct can remain stable once it is articulated, even when an articulation of masculinity is invested with power by virtue of its official status. When masculinity is viewed as an imposed form of power, then the imposition of power necessarily leads to resistance against it, even as that resistance may or may not be outside the original field of power."

another, within or beyond a country's borders.[19] In this case, the priests perform religious rituals, connecting the people to God, and receive foodstuffs in exchange. Resource flow, however, is not just about economics. A society's structure determines what goes where and to whom.[20] While flow charts can be circular, social structures are often both vertical and horizontal, and the priests stand at the head of the religious line in Malachi's community. Their duties supposedly cannot be performed by anyone else, giving them power and authority to demand the fruits, carbohydrates, and protein that are their due.

In a society of limited resources, however, the flow chart can break down. In Belize, for example, the *dugu* ceremony, performed on behalf of the seriously ill and designed to appease their ancestors, requires the sacrifice of numerous fowl (all male), plus the occasional male pig.[21] Most of the food goes to the living guests and not the dead ancestors; anthropologist Carol Jenkins notes, "Since it is the living who give voice to the wishes of the ancestors, increased demands for sharing are clearly an expression of contemporary social stresses."[22] Occasionally, the ancestors call for a new temple as well. The *dugu* ceremony celebrated by the Garifuna in modern Belize and the understanding of resource flow both illuminate rhetorical elements in Haggai and Malachi. Just as the biblical prophet speaks for God, the *buyai*, or shaman, speaks for the ancestors, and like Haggai's God, the ancestors may insist upon the construction of a new temple, where the people share as opposed to hoard their resources.[23] While this system reaches a crisis point in Malachi, in both biblical books and among the Garifuna, the cultures' spirits insist upon respect, which the people tangibly deliver through sacrifices of time and financial resources.

In the following chapters, I will expand upon Haggai's and Malachi's portrayal of the image of God as a threatening complainer, willing to

19. Josephine Smart, "The Global Economy and South China Development in Post–1978 China: Relevance and Limitations of the Flexible Accumulation Approach," *Urban Anthropology* 28 (1999): 412. Food chain may be the more common term, but resource flow (unlike the food chain) addresses more than food. And Malachi's connection of the flow (or lack thereof) to blessings and curses fits more within the description of resource flow.

20. Ibid., 422.

21. Carol L. Jenkins, "Ritual and Resource Flow: The Garifuna 'Dugu,'" *American Ethnologist* 10 (1983): 433–34.

22. Ibid., 435.

23. Ibid., 433, 435–36.

starve or burn his children into submission, because this portrayal raises important exegetical and theological issues. Each chapter functions as a critical reflection/meditation upon the biblical text. Using the work of other scholars and my own scholarly senses, I describe what I think the text means, occasionally asking more questions than I can answer. This approach is deliberate. Rhetorical and feminist critics (and I am both) argue for the inevitability and the recognition of subjectivity. In her essay on rhetorical criticism, Patricia K. Tull notes that "when contexts change, interpretation is altered."[24] In other words, what a biblical text may have meant 2,500 years ago may not be what it means today. Rhetorical critics reject the idea of "*the* meaning" of a text, instead suggesting that a text may mean a number of things. Not even rhetorical criticism has a single meaning.[25] Furthermore, feminist critic Julia M. O'Brien states that our lives, personal and professional, influence our scholarship.[26] She writes, "Evaluative discourse implies an evaluator whose personal, historical, and social circumstances influence the evaluation, and to fail to acknowledge the power of the personal paradoxically grants it ultimate power—*uncontested* power."[27] As such, I make no claims for either personal objectivity or exegetical definitiveness. Anthropologist Clifford Geertz reminds scholars that the study of another culture is an incomplete art as well as a social science; uncertainty remains inevitable, and the work depends on a scholar's best educated guesses. Charles Segal, however, notes that "some readings [of a text] may be better than others."[28] I have tried to offer textually accurate readings here.

The interpretations of Haggai and Malachi belong to me and represent only me, being neither the first nor the last word on the texts. Instead, they are a "contribution to an ongoing conversation."[29] And I am blessed

24. Tull, "Rhetorical Criticism," 158.

25. Ibid., 168.

26. Julia M. O'Brien, "On Saying 'No' to a Prophet," in *Prophets and Daniel: A Feminist Companion to the Prophets*, ed. Athalya Brenner, FCB 2/8 (Sheffield: Sheffield Academic Press, 2001), 214–16.

27. Ibid., 215.

28. Clifford Geertz, *The Interpretation of Cultures: Selected Essays* (New York: Basic Books, 1973), 25, 29; Charles Segal, *Interpreting Greek Tragedy: Myth, Poetry, Text* (Ithaca, NY: Cornell UP, 1986), 370.

29. The quotation comes from Professor Molly Gower during a department colloquium on April 10, 2014, in which this introduction was the topic of conversation. I thank her for the insight, which helped me clarify what I mean regarding objectivity and definiteness.

enough to have friends in the fields of sociology and theology who are Jewish, Christian, and secular contributing to this volume. Their voices make this work a stronger example of rhetorical and feminist commentary. O'Brien noted almost twenty years ago that "despite the growth of feminist and postmodern interpretations in the academy as a whole, these perspectives have not yet surfaced significantly in Malachi studies."[30] Haggai can be accurately substituted for Malachi in the previous sentence. The number of feminist sources on both books remains small. So, this volume not only adds to the number but also seeks to inspire many more.

30. Julia M. O'Brien, "Malachi in Recent Research," *CurBS* 3 (1995): 90.

Haggai 1:1-15

The Art of Persuasion

Haggai's first prophetic words offer a plain message of negative divine retribution—God punishes the disobedient. The community's failure to begin reconstruction of the temple has caused significant financial hardship. Haggai insists that the people must rebuild the temple in order to rebuild their own economy. Although the prophet argues simply, directly, and at length in Hag 1:1-12, his words do not elicit a simple, direct, or quick response. Haggai then utters another prophecy in 1:13, and more divine activity takes place before the reconstruction project gets underway. Haggai's words achieve their intended purpose, but not immediately. This suggests that the people earnestly "consider how [they] have fared" (Hag 1:5, 7) and ponder the "word of the Lord" (Hag 1:1). They take their time, making time itself—specifically when to act—a significant theme in the passage.

Haggai's activity begins "in the second year of King Darius, in the sixth month, on the first day of the month" (1:1). The date corresponds to the beginning of Elul, or August/September 520. The only other books that begin with such a precise date marker are Ezekiel and Zechariah, and, with only one exception, each of Haggai's prophecies takes place on a specific day. So, time clearly matters to the prophet. But why is this particular time important?

Haggai goes to Zerubbabel the governor and Joshua the high priest, the political and religious leaders, with a message about time: "Thus says the Lord of hosts: These people say *the time* has not yet come to

Hag 1:1-15

[1]In the second year of King Darius,
in the sixth month, on the first day of
the month, the word of the Lord came
by the prophet Haggai to Zerubbabel
son of Shealtiel, governor of Judah,
and to Joshua son of Jehozadak, the
high priest: [2]Thus says the LORD of
hosts: These people say the time has
not yet come to rebuild the LORD's
house. [3]Then the word of the LORD
came by the prophet Haggai, saying:
[4]Is it a time for you yourselves to live
in your paneled houses, while this
house lies in ruins? [5]Now therefore
thus says the LORD of hosts: Consider
how you have fared. [6]You have sown
much, and harvested little; you eat, but
you never have enough; you drink, but
you never have your fill; you clothe
yourselves, but no one is warm; and
you that earn wages earn wages to put
them into a bag with holes.

[7]Thus says the LORD of hosts: Con-
sider how you have fared. [8]Go up to the
hills and bring wood and build the
house, so that I may take pleasure in it
and be honored, says the LORD. [9]You
have looked for much, and, lo, it came
to little; and when you brought it home,
I blew it away. Why? says the LORD of

rebuild the Lord's house" (1:2; emphasis mine). Almost twenty years have passed since the exile's end in 539 BCE, but the people are still not ready to take on the project of restoring the temple, according to the prophet. Opposing delay, Haggai retorts, "Is it a time for you yourselves to live in your *paneled* houses, while this house lies in ruins?" (1:4; emphasis mine). The Hebrew word ספן, translated as "paneled" in the NRSV, literally means "to cover, cover in"; "panel" is the third definition, and it suggests a decorated, elaborate home.[1] Covered houses, however, are basic, plain structures that have roofs. The distinction matters. If the people's houses are paneled, then they have disposable income that could be used to improve the dreadful state of God's house. If the houses are only covered, then the people are barely getting by and may be justifiably disinclined to take on the temple project, with its demands upon time and treasure. Based on Haggai's description of the people's circumstances in verses 6 and 9-11, the houses appear to be only roofed[2] as opposed to paneled in cedar.[3] The people observe their economic situa-

1. BDB, 706.

2. John Kessler, *The Book of Haggai: Prophecy and Society in Early Persian Yehud* (Leiden: Brill, 2002), 128; Janet E. Tollington, *Tradition and Innovation in Haggai and Zechariah 1–8* (Sheffield: JSOT, 1993), 183.

3. David L. Petersen, *Haggai and Zechariah 1–8: A Commentary* (Philadelphia: Westminster, 1984), 48, 50.

hosts. Because my house lies in ruins, while all of you hurry off to your own houses. [10]Therefore the heavens above you have withheld the dew, and the earth has withheld its produce. [11]And I have called for a drought on the land and the hills, on the grain, the new wine, the oil, on what the soil produces, on human beings and animals, and on all their labors.

[12]Then Zerubbabel son of Shealtiel, and Joshua son of Jehozadak, the high priest, with all the remnant of the people, obeyed the voice of the LORD their God, and the words of the prophet Haggai, as the LORD their God had sent him; and the people feared the LORD. [13]Then Haggai, the messenger of the LORD, spoke to the people with the LORD's message, saying, I am with you, says the LORD. [14]And the LORD stirred up the spirit of Zerubbabel son of Shealtiel, governor of Judah, and the spirit of Joshua son of Jehozadak, the high priest, and the spirit of all the remnant of the people; and they came and worked on the house of the LORD of hosts their God, [15]on the twenty-fourth day of the month, in the sixth month.

tion—poor crop yields, lack of adequate food and clothing, drought, and "the problem of inflation"[4]—and conclude that they cannot afford to rebuild the temple at this time.[5] The phrase "paneled houses" may therefore be hyperbole or a reference to the homes of the wealthy few,[6] but the majority is not as fortunate.

A number of scholars argue that the people hesitate to rebuild because they are unsure if the theological time is right. Has God's anger subsided enough for the people to restore the house destroyed by that anger? Has God ended God's rejection of the people?[7] This argument, however, has

4. Tollington, *Tradition and Innovation*, 188.

5. Willem S. Prinsloo, "The Cohesion of Haggai 1:4-11," in *"Wünschet Jerusalem Frieden": Collected Communications to the XIIth Congress of the International Organization for the Study of the Old Testament, Jerusalem 1986*, ed. Matthias Augustin and Klaus-Dietrich Schunck (Frankfurt am Main: Peter Lang, 1988), 340; John Kessler, "Building the Second Temple: Questions of Time, Text, and History in Haggai 1.1-15," *JSOT* 27 (2002): 243–56.

6. Paul L. Redditt, *Haggai, Zechariah, Malachi* (Grand Rapids, MI: Eerdmans, 1995), 19.

7. Elie Assis, "Composition, Rhetoric and Theology in Haggai 1:1-11," *JHebS* 7 (2007): 3, 13–14. Elie Assis, "To Build or Not to Build: A Dispute between Haggai and His People (Hag 1)," *ZAW* 119 (2007): 517–18; Hayim Tadmor, " 'The Appointed Time Has Not Yet Arrived': The Historical Background of Haggai 1:2," in *Ki Baruch Hu: Ancient Near Eastern, Biblical and Judaic Studies in Honor of Baruch A. Levine*, ed. Robert Chazan, William W. Hallo, and Lawrence H. Schiffman (Winona Lake, IN: Eisenbrauns,

one problem: the rest of Haggai's prophecy does not support it. If the people's delay comes from uncertainty about their standing with God, then Haggai's words should be reassuring. Yet the reassurance ("I am with you" in Hag 1:13) comes only after the prophet criticizes the people twice about the ruined temple in comparison to the people's homes. Additionally, Haggai's emphasis upon the state of the economy suggests that the people's concerns about rebuilding, or at least Haggai's understanding of those concerns, are financial. If the prophet therefore can convince Zerubbabel and Joshua that everyone's economic woes stem from a failure to rebuild the temple, then his goal will be met. And that is exactly what eventually happens.

The Call to Rebuild the Church: Reading Haggai in the Pontificate of Pope Francis, Part 1

Images of a church in a town in the province of Pampanga near my home in the Philippines kept coming to mind. This church was rebuilt or more accurately updated the year after the eruption of Mt. Pinatubo when massive lahar flow and flooding affected a large segment of the province. Lahar would bury whole towns and take many lives over the course of years, changing the typography of the region. I had family members and friends lose homes and loved ones because of this disaster. And here was this church, which stood on the edge of this calamity, rebuilt at the cost of millions of pesos while so many were forced into evacuation centers, wanting for the most basic of necessities. What was most stark is not that a church ought to be constructed during such times. After all, so many historic churches were lost. Many would have welcomed the building of such a place for prayer and worship. But, somehow, those who planned its construction decided that they would paint the entire sanctuary gold. And the sight of this left a sick feeling in my stomach.

As news continued to be broadcasted over radio and television about more homes being lost and people living in

1999), 405–6; Frank Y. Patrick, "Time and Tradition in the Book of Haggai," in *Tradition in Transition: Haggai and Zechariah 1–8 in the Trajectory of Hebrew Theology*, ed. Mark J. Boda and Michael H. Floyd (New York: T & T Clark, 2008), 41, 47; Peter Ross Bedford, "Discerning the Time: Haggai, Zechariah, and the 'Delay' in the Rebuilding of the Jerusalem Temple," in *The Pitcher Is Broken: Memorial Essays for Gösta W. Ahlström*, ed. Steven W. Holloway and Lowell K. Handy (Sheffield: Sheffield Academic, 1995), 74–75.

makeshift evacuation centers, this church was being built.

Now I must confess that I knew nothing of the circumstances of the construction of this building beyond what I saw. All I am sure of is what I felt when I walked in from the rain to pray for people living in the path of the lahar. I was shocked and astounded, sickened by this expression of faith in the midst of so much suffering at its doorstep.

Each time I read Haggai, this image would come to me. A god who would ask the people to build a church with a golden sanctuary would invade my thoughts and prayers and repulse me. Each time, all I could read from the book of the prophet was this story of a god who demanded that the people first rebuild the physical temple before attending to the needs of the people. I did not want to find this god in the sacred text of my faith. I did not want to find in the sacred text a prophet who would justify temple worship as taking precedence over the needs of the people, the cry of the poor.

There had to be a way out. The deity being described could not be the God of Haggai, the God of Israel. I must have misunderstood, and so I turned to scholarship. I looked for commentaries and introductions to the book of the prophet, and no introduction or commentary helped. I could not see beyond the interpretation that I had already constructed. I had no way of seeing beyond the image of a god who wanted the rebuilding of the temple before rebuilding the homes of the homeless. And I could not write about this god, so I did not write. I stopped reading Haggai. I stopped trying to pray with Haggai.

Time passed. The Catholic world came on fire with the election of Jorge Mario Bergoglio, the first Jesuit pope, the first pope from Latin America, from the two-thirds world. This was exciting enough in and of itself. That these elements of his social location actually meant something, that is, that they actually manifested themselves in the way he leads, is nothing less than a sign of the Spirit at work in the church.

The work began with a rather timid looking man making his way to the balcony of St. Peter's Basilica to stand before the gathered crowd awaiting the presentation of the new pope. When his name was announced, there was simultaneous excitement and a bit of confusion as many did not know who this was. As he stepped out dressed in simple white, setting aside the appearance of a monarch greeting his people, many began to become aware that there was something different happening here. When people heard he had taken on the name Francis, many speculated that he was evoking one of the first Jesuits, St. Francis Xavier, an original companion of St. Ignatius of Loyola. But people would soon learn that it was not the Jesuit saint but St. Francis of Assisi that was his namesake. This created even greater excitement. He dared take on the name Francis. No one had done that!

After a year of Pope Francis, this man who took on the name of Francis of Assisi to remind himself always of the poor and forgotten of the world, I reread Haggai. In that text, I now find an invitation to my church, to my community, to me. I understood why God admonishes the people for tending to their houses before the house of God. Calling upon the people to tend first to the temple, to the place where they encounter God, to the place where they could properly give thanks and to cry out for their needs, made sense. It is to this invitation and this challenge of Haggai to the church that I will turn.

Catherine Punsalan-Manlimos

Whether the delay is self-interested or theological matters not to Haggai; the ruined temple stands as an insult to God, and God responds. According to Haggai, the people suffer lack—substandard harvests, hunger, thirst, and inadequate clothing. Wage earners "earn wages to put them into a bag with holes" (Hag 1:6); their money lacks value. After asking the people twice to "consider how you have fared" (Hag 1:5, 7), Haggai gives this order: "Go up to the hills and bring wood and build the house, so that I may take pleasure in it and be honored, says the Lord" (1:8). Because God has been displeased and dishonored, God says, "You have looked for much and lo, it came to little; and when you brought it home, I blew it away" (Hag 1:9). The people's dire economic situation, exacerbated by a lack of rain, comes from God's word: "And I have called for a drought on the land and the hills, on the grain, the new wine, the oil, on what the soil produces, on human beings and animals, and on all their labors" (Hag 1:11). Just as in Hosea, where people's actions cause misery to animals (4:3), failure to rebuild the temple results in environmental degradation.

If the community desires an end to this trouble and the beginning of better days, then they must meet God's desire and rebuild God's dilapidated house.[8] John Kessler persuasively argues that the call to rebuild should be understood in "the sense of simple succession, that is the expression of a promise of acceptance," as opposed to building the

8. Redditt, *Haggai, Zechariah, Malachi*, 20.

temple "so that one [God] might accept it."[9] While the NRSV translates Hag 1:8b as "so that I may take pleasure in it and be honored," the Hebrew ו, translated as "so that" literally is "and," supporting Kessler's contention that the conjunction does not have to be translated consecutively. Kessler calls the verse "a promise of salvation,"[10] but Paul Redditt is more reserved, suggesting only that the verse is eschatological; if the building project takes place, then the people will see better days.[11] Both suggestions, however, assume the principle of positive divine retribution. If the temple reconstruction will make God happy, then a happy God will make the people happy, or at least call off the drought.

At the conclusion of Haggai's first word from the Lord, not only do Zerubbabel and Joshua respond with obedience to and respect for God, but "all the remnant of the people" do as well (1:12). While the message's audience is the governor and the high priest, it affects everyone in the area. Therefore, "remnant" in this context means all people[12] as opposed to Ezra's description of the remnant as only the returned exiles from Babylon (Ezra 9:15). The obedient people, however, do not respond to Haggai's first prophecy.

In fact, further divine activity is required. The people accept "the words of the prophet Haggai, as the LORD their God had sent him" (Hag 1:12), but they do not start gathering wood. Janet Tollington suggests that Haggai's argumentation about divine retribution gives his listeners space to make their own decision, concluding "this may have some bearing on why the people responded to Haggai's preaching while the message of earlier prophets frequently went unheeded."[13] And the community responds deliberately. Not even Haggai's claim that God wreaks havoc with the people's livelihood on account of the ruined temple makes them move faster. The people's own homes and lives are in fragile shape, and the temple simply has not been a priority. Haggai describes God as peeved about the temple, but God's "What about my house?" does not lead to instant action. So, Haggai then receives a second message at some unspecified time after the first day of the month; this message is "to the people," not just Zerubbabel and Joshua (1:13). The message is brief: "I am with you, says the LORD" (Hag 1:13). "The people

9. Kessler, *Book of Haggai*, 135.

10. Ibid., 110.

11. Redditt, *Haggai, Zechariah, Malachi*, 20.

12. Ibid., 22; Kessler, *Book of Haggai*, 141–42; Petersen, *Haggai and Zechariah* 1–8, 47.

13. Tollington, *Tradition and Innovation*, 192.

feared the LORD," but that fear did not spur them to immediate action (Hag 1:12). Neither does Haggai's new message.

Before work on the temple finally begins, "the LORD stirred up the spirit of Zerubbabel son of Shealtiel, governor of Judah, and the spirit of Joshua son of Jehozadak, the high priest, and the spirit of all the remnant of the people" (Hag 1:14). W. Sibley Towner thinks that Haggai's "I am with you" (1:13) "results in stirred up spirits,"[14] but no textual reason exists for Hag 1:14 to be the result of the previous verse, as Towner suggests, or to be a summary/conclusion of the preceding verses.[15] Instead, Haggai speaks, and then God works.[16] David L. Petersen notes, "Despite the presumed effectiveness of Haggai's words, Yahweh intervened to force the people to action."[17] Force, however, may be too strong a verb. In Hebrew, the verb עור , translated in the NRSV as "to stir up," literally means "to awake."[18] After years of neglecting the temple, or being asleep, the people are awakened by God, and they begin to work.

A Feminist Review of Haggai and the Building of the Second Temple

From the standpoint of a sociologist and a feminist scholar of Africana studies, Haggai is striking in three important ways: (1) the sociopolitical context in which the book is written and the exilic experience of dislocated people; (2) the explicit and latent patriarchy, as demonstrated in the omission of women and in the presentation of men; and (3) the verse itself, specifically Haggai's appeal to the people of Judah to rebuild the destroyed temple and the threat of holy retribution if they do not.

Haggai, named for the prophet who composed it, is situated in a fascinating era and geographical place. The book is dated in the opening line of the first verse by its reference to King Darius I, who was the ruling monarch over the Persian Empire. The Persian Kingdom, at the time, expanded across three continents—Asia, Africa, and Europe—and by today's standards such a kingdom would be considered a geopolitical superpower. To understand the significance of

14. W. Sibley Towner, "Haggai," in *The Harper Collins Study Bible, Fully Revised and Updated*, ed. Harold W. Attridge (San Francisco: HarperSanFrancisco, 2006), 1265.

15. Kessler, *Book of Haggai*, 150–51.

16. Assis, "To Build or Not to Build," 525–26.

17. Petersen, *Haggai and Zechariah 1–8*, 58.

18. BDB 734.

Haggai's reference to King Darius I, it is important to discuss, in brief, how Darius ascended to power.

The Persian Empire that Darius I eventually inherits is more or less built on the legacy of King Cyrus, also known as Cyrus the Great, who is sometimes referred to as the "founder" of the Persian Empire.[19] Cyrus the Great's reign over Persia began in 558 BCE and lasted until his death in 530 BCE. As the king of Persia, one of Cyrus's most notorious achievements was the military capture of Babylon and the subsequent liberation of Jewish exiles in 538 BCE. The people of Judah had been taken into captivity in Babylon between 597 and 582 BCE. In the process of conquering the Judeans, Nebuchadnezzar II, the ruling king of Babylon, destroyed their land and holy temple. At King Cyrus's death, his son Cambyses II rose to power in 530 BCE and ruled the Persian Empire until his death in 522 BCE. For one year, between 522 and 521 BCE, an imposter named King Gaumata ruled Persia. Impersonating King Cyrus's other son, Smerdish, who incidentally had been beheaded at the orders of his brother King Cambyses, Gaumata appointed himself king. Darius I and six other noblemen removed him from power and killed him at once. Darius I then succeeded as the next ruler of Persia and presided as such from 521 to 486 BCE. It is here that the book of Haggai begins.

In the first line of the first verse, following the reference to King Darius I, Haggai continues: "The word of the LORD came by the prophet Haggai to Zerubbabel, son of Shealtiel, governor of Judah, and to Joshua, son of Jehozadak, the high priest" (1:1). The reference to Zerubbabel, the governor of Judah, and Joshua, the high priest, reflects King Darius's decentralizing political approach. King Darius organized his vast empire into centralized provinces that were locally administered by *Khshathrapavans* or *satraps*.[20] These "satraps" or governors basically served as liaisons between the king and the local populace under his rule. King Darius had selected the governor Zerubbabel to oversee the reestablishment of Judah and, along with Joshua the high priest, the rebuilding of the holy temple.

The prophet Haggai makes an appeal to the overseers of two of the most influential and powerful social institutions in Judah: the government and the religious authorities. Frustrated by the stalled progress in efforts to rebuild the temple, Haggai

19. Samuel G. Benjamin, *Persia* (London: T. Fisher Unwin Ltd, 1920), 86.
20. Ibid., 104.

tells the governor, Zerubbabel, and the high priest, Joshua, that the Lord is dissatisfied. Haggai, who is clearly frustrated with the contradictions and inaction of the returnees, rebukes them for having yielded too little in return for their efforts. As such, he calls on them to give cautionary thought to their unpleasing ways.

The power dynamics among the prophet, the governor, and the high priest are striking. Perhaps sociologist C. Wright Mills would have characterized this collection of men, the highest authorities in the most prominent social institutions of Judah, as an emerging or emerged Power Elite who convened with a common purpose to ensure that the temple would be reconstructed. In addition, it is important to note that God chose to communicate through Haggai: not a woman, not a commoner, but a male prophet who, presumably, had unfettered access to the city's highest authorities.

The presentation of men not only in the biblical book of Haggai but also in scholarly texts that address the history of the Persian Empire reflects the deep-rooted patriarchal social arrangement that was staunchly present in this era. Women, when noted, are mentioned in reference to their relationship to men as either mothers of sons or wives of husbands;[21] usually, however, they are simply omitted from reference all together. When men are presented, they too are customarily introduced in relationship to other men, usually their fathers, such as Zerubbabel "son of Shealtiel" and Joshua "son of Jehozadak," mentioned in three places in this very short book of Haggai.

The prophet tells the people to go into the mountains to retrieve materials to build the Lord's house, so that he could be honored. Haggai's message is fiercely angry and effectively evokes a warning of holy retribution. According to the prophet, the Lord communicates through him to the people of Judah. Because the people feared God, they obeyed the prophet's message, but the reconstruction of the temple did not commence immediately. So, the prophet was given a second message to deliver. Accordingly, the Lord declares "I am with you." This message inspires Zerubbabel, Joshua, and the "remnant of the people" into action, and on the twenty-fourth day of the sixth month in the second year of King Darius's rule of Persia, the second holy temple is begun.

Carolette Norwood

21. Jacob Abbott, *History of Cyrus The Great* (New York: Harper & Brothers, 1850); Benjamin, *Persia*.

Certain scholars describe the people's response to Haggai's words as speedy. According to Kessler, "the dating formula in 15a serves to indicate the rapidity with which the resumption of the work was undertaken."[22] Carol L. Meyers and Eric M. Meyers claim that "the response of all sectors of the community to Haggai's plea is immediate and unanimous,"[23] but an instantaneous reaction to the rebuilding call does not appear to be the case. Haggai prophesies on the first day of the month. Zerubbabel, Joshua, and the remnant "came and worked on the house of the Lord of hosts, their God, on the twenty-fourth day of the month, in the sixth month" (Hag 1:14-15). Three and a half weeks pass between the prophetic word and the called-for action, so this response by definition is not immediate, or "following or preceding without a lapse of time."[24] Redditt notes the time lag without comment. Meyers and Meyers, after suggesting that the people may have needed time to think, still conclude that "the preliminary work on the temple site began immediately."[25]

The biblical text, however, suggests that the people wake up slowly. Haggai's initial insistence upon taking care of God's house takes an entire chapter to come to fruition, but the delay need not be interpreted negatively or ignored entirely. Instead, the delay shows that the people can and do think for themselves. Just because a prophet says God is unhappy does not mean it is so. Plus, the people apparently do not make the connection between farming trouble and the neglected temple as quickly as Haggai does. In spite of the twenty-three-day gap between Haggai's first message and the commencement of the people's work, though, God sends no more sharp messages through the prophet. The people may have houses, and God does not have one; but God has told them that twice already, without success.

While the people are slow, God is patient. Another prophetic message and a metaphorical tap on the shoulder get them moving. Haggai 1 shows a relationship between God and the community in which the

22. Kessler, *Book of Haggai*, 153.

23. Carol L. Meyers and Eric M. Meyers, *Haggai, Zechariah 1–8, A New Translation with Introduction and Commentary*, AB 25B (New York: Doubleday, 1987), 43.

24. Dictionary.com Unabridged, s.v. "immediate," Random House, Inc., last modified February 2015, http://dictionary.reference.com/browse/immediate; David L. Petersen concludes that the people did *not* spring immediately to action (*Haggai and Zechariah 1–8*, 58, 60).

25. Meyers and Meyers, *Haggai, Zechariah 1–8*, 46.

pristine house in which only a few can dwell.

> "Now thus says the LORD of hosts: Consider your ways! You have sown much, but brought in little; you have eaten but have not been satisfied." (Hag 1:5-6)

Rather:

> "Consider your ways! Go up into the hill country; bring timber, and build the house that I may take pleasure in it and receive my glory, says the Lord." (Hag 1:7-8)

The image of "going up" reminds me of Pope Francis's invitation. He calls upon the church not only to open its doors so that people may enter. Rather, he challenges the people in the church to pass through those doors and go out into the world. There they can tend to the needs of people and in so doing bring the gospel to life. This is the rebuilding of the temple that is needed in our times. So many among us and around us are lost and feel alone, abandoned and forgotten.

St. Francis of Assisi rebuilt the church of St. Damian by carrying one stone at a time piece by piece, but he helped rebuild the larger church by choosing to live a life of voluntary poverty devoted to caring for the poor. His example of a life of voluntary poverty restored the church and served as a reminder of the good news of divine love for humanity preached by Jesus, a love that was incarnate in the manger. Pope Francis, like this saint, calls on us to rebuild the church by going out into the world. He challenges shepherds of the church to have the "smell of the sheep." He calls on the whole church to become "a poor church for the poor."

In rereading the prophet Haggai in the pontificate of Pope Francis, I heard Haggai's accusation that the people were tending to their own houses and neglecting the temple spoken against the backdrop of a church that has become self-referential and has forgotten to listen to the cry of God's people. In this context, I now hear God's command to rebuild the temple, to rebuild the church so that it may once again be a place where people may worship and encounter God.

Catherine Punsalan-Manlimos

Haggai 2:1-9

God as "The Man"

Having rallied the people for the rebuilding of the temple in his previous prophecies, Haggai continues to encourage the construction work. "I am with you, says the LORD," both in Hag 1:13 and in 2:4. The concern about divine status and honor reappears as well. The temple may seem insignificant now, but God will make it glorious in the future using other nations' money. Not only will God finally have a house but that house also will be much more luxurious than the Israelites' "paneled houses" about which God complains in Hag 1:4. This eschatological prophecy often receives a positive or at least a benign interpretation, but the prophecy's language suggests a less than pleasant scenario. The temple's and, therefore, God's future glory results from a divinely initiated shakedown of the nations, a reassertion of God's power that may have been questioned because of the exile.

Almost a month after rebuilding begins, Haggai prophesies in response to what is often described as the people's complaints about the temple. Haggai asks, "Who is left among you that saw this house in its former glory? How does it look to you now? Is it not in your sight as nothing?" (2:3). Scholars characterize these questions as the people's "derision of the Temple"[1] or their "ridicule of the building project."[2]

1. Elie Assis, "A Disputed Temple (Haggai 2, 1-9)," *ZAW* 120 (2008): 583.
2. Paul L. Redditt, *Haggai, Zechariah, Malachi* (Grand Rapids, MI: Eerdmans, 1995), 24.

Hag 2:1-9

In the second year of King Darius, [1]in the seventh month, on the twenty-first day of the month, the word of the LORD came by the prophet Haggai, saying: [2]Speak now to Zerubbabel son of Shealtiel, governor of Judah, and to Joshua son of Jehozadak, the high priest, and to the remnant of the people, and say, [3]Who is left among you that saw this house in its former glory? How does it look to you now? Is it not in your sight as nothing? [4]Yet now take courage, O Zerubbabel, says the LORD; take courage, O Joshua, son of Jehozadak, the high priest; take courage, all you people of the land, says the LORD; work, for I am with you, says the LORD of hosts, [5]according to the promise that I made you when you came out of Egypt. My spirit abides among you; do not fear. [6]For thus says the LORD of hosts: Once again, in a little while, I will shake the heavens and the earth and the sea and the dry land; [7]and I will shake all the nations, so that the treasure of all nations shall come, and I will fill this house with splendor, says the LORD of hosts. [8]The silver is mine, and the gold is mine, says the LORD of hosts. [9]The latter splendor of this house shall be greater than the former, says the LORD of hosts; and in this place I will give prosperity, says the LORD of hosts.

John Kessler concludes that the people see the temple as without value, and Carol L. and Eric M. Meyers concur—because the builders are poor and powerless, the building will be too.[3] The complaints focus less on the building's physical structure; practically, one month of work cannot a magnificent temple make.[4] Instead, Elie Assis suggests that just as in Hag 1, the people question whether now is the time to build.[5] Does God support their efforts?

According to Haggai, the answer is yes. The prophet exhorts Zerubbabel, Joshua, and the people to "take courage" (Hag 2:4). The Hebrew root is חזק, often translated as "to be strong." Everyone can continue to be strong and build because God says, "My spirit abides with you; do not fear" (Hag 2:5). God favored the Exodus generation, which built the tabernacle; so too God favors this generation and its rebuilding of the temple.[6] David L. Petersen notes that Haggai speaks of the end of Sukkot, the festival

3. John Kessler, *The Book of Haggai: Prophecy and Society in Early Persian Yehud* (Leiden: Brill, 2002), 166; Carol L. Meyers and Eric M. Meyers, *Haggai, Zechariah 1–8, A New Translation with Introduction and Commentary*, AB 25B (New York: Doubleday, 1987), 72.

4. Kessler, *Book of Haggai*, 167.

5. Assis, "A Disputed Temple," 588–89.

6. Max Rogland, "Text and Temple in Haggai 2, 5," *ZAW* 119 (2007): 414–15.

that commemorates the wilderness experience following the exodus; the reference to Egypt intentionally recalls that time of God's goodwill and deliverance.[7] The prophet's exhortation could have ended here, but instead it offers a glimpse of the future.

The eschatological vision of Hag 2:6-9 reiterates the fact that God supports the reconstruction of the temple. Kessler states that the themes of shaking, "the enriching of the temple, and eschatological peace are stock components of a common eschatological scenario deeply rooted in Israelite traditions."[8] As Paul L. Redditt observes, however, the passage functions politically as well as eschatologically.[9] According to Haggai, God says, "I will shake the nations" and the people in them, "so that the treasure of all nations shall come" (Hag 2:7). This demonstration of divine power (the shaking of the earth) terrifies the earth's people, who also shake.[10]

The relevance of the shaking and consequent tribute paying remains a topic of debate. Petersen suggests that the treasure refers to the temple vessels taken in 587/86, "and their return was a necessary part of a proper restoration."[11] Meyers and Meyers view the shaking as a good deed, even though the nations must pay God tribute; they write, "Both clauses ('all nations will arrive with riches' and 'thus I will fill this house with glory') inform us of the positive consequences of God's 'shaking' the world."[12] Max Rogland entirely neglects the nations' plundering. For him, "this promise of a great abundance of wealth coming into the Temple hearkens [*sic*] back to the Exodus narrative, in which the people were commanded to offer valuable materials such as silver and gold and generously responded."[13] The challenge with this reading is that Hag 2:7 does not state that the builders of the temple will have their pockets emptied of loose change; instead, this will happen to כל־גוים ("all the nations"), presumably non-Israelites. Therefore, the text is related more to Exod 11:1-2, 12:33-36, in which the Israelites leave slavery with gold, silver, and clothing from the Egyptians. The Israelites' financial contributions to the tabernacle are at least in part a result of their having

7. Petersen, *Haggai and Zechariah 1–8*, 62, 66.
8. Kessler, *Book of Haggai*, 185.
9. Redditt, *Haggai, Zechariah, Malachi*, 25.
10. Kessler, *Book of Haggai*, 176, 78.
11. Petersen, *Haggai and Zechariah 1–8*, 68.
12. Meyers and Meyers, *Haggai, Zechariah 1–8*, 53.
13. Rogland, "Text and Temple," 414.

"plundered the Egyptians" (Exod 12:36). If sacred space is created at another's expense, then is the space's sanctity questionable?

Haggai 2:6-9 is often read from an Israelite perspective, but examining Israelite eschatology from the other nations' point of view destabilizes a positive assessment of the text. Meyers and Meyers conclude that "the power of Yahweh as universal ruler will not be exploitative"[14] and that the shaking of the nations is nothing in comparison with Hag 2:21-22, "in which the result is calamitous for the other nations."[15] By definition, however, exploit means "to utilize, esp. for profit; turn to practical account . . . to use selfishly for one's own ends," according to the *Random House Dictionary*. Since the nations' treasure will be used for God's purposes and not their own, specifically the glorification of the temple, the shaking of the nations is exploitative. Also, being forcibly bankrupted in order to finance someone else's building project may be disastrous for the victim of that shakedown. First Kings 5:13 states that "forced labor" built the first temple; tribute will build the second temple. Kessler argues that, while Hag 2 uses several eschatological images that emphasize war and combat, less violent images also appear, including the gathering of treasure.[16] If the gathering comes directly from the shaking, however, then the image is violent.

Kessler claims that the text cannot be excessively bellicose, since it lacks a discussion of "the subjugation of non-Jews. . . . The role of the Gentile nations vis-à-vis Israel and Yahweh is left undefined, despite the reference to the treasures of those nations."[17] However, this is not quite the case. At a minimum, the Gentiles become a source of loot for the temple, a less than pacific image. God appears as the enforcer who literally shakes other nations and takes whatever spoils happen to fall. Isaiah 23:17-18, the conclusion of the oracle against Tyre, reads as follows:

> At the end of seventy years, the LORD will visit Tyre, and she will return to her trade, and will prostitute herself with all the kingdoms of the world on the face of the earth. Her merchandise and her wages will be dedicated to the LORD; her profits will not be stored or hoarded, but her merchandise will supply abundant food and fine clothing for those who live in the presence of the LORD.

14. Meyers and Meyers, *Haggai, Zechariah 1–8*, 75.
15. Ibid., 53.
16. Kessler, *Book of Haggai*, 188.
17. Ibid., 195.

God acts as a pimp here, securing Tyre's income not for Tyre's benefit but for God's own people. Recent feminist research on food and environmental justice and consumer culture challenges readers and listeners to question carefully where goods come from and who benefits (or does not benefit) from the making and acquisition of those goods.[18] The same questions should be asked about the temple's stockpile of treasure.

Once the treasure arrives, "I will fill this house with splendor, says the LORD of hosts" (Hag 2:7). What is the source of the glory or כבוד ("splendor")? For Kessler, it is God. When language about treasure and references to worship appear in the same passage, they focus more on the deity and less on the treasure.[19] Kessler argues as follows: "Thus, in Hag 2.7, כבוד is more specifically the splendor or honour that is the result of the presence of the nations' riches offered to Yahweh, rather than the riches themselves."[20] Petersen takes the opposite approach: "The possessions, rather than God, will provide *kābôd* [glory or splendor]."[21] Feminist theory challenges binary thinking and argumentation;[22] therefore, if applied to Hag 2:7 and the following verse, then both God and the riches are the source of glory. God boasts, "The silver is mine, and the gold is mine" (Hag 2:8). Therefore, God claims the power to appropriate anyone's wealth for his own glorification and his own house. With construction finally underway, God wants the house to be a beautiful structure, a reflection of the deity who will be honored there. According to the theory of divine retribution, obeying God leads to wealth (Deut 28:1-14). Consequently, God's house should look extravagant, perhaps even gaudy. Haggai concludes, "The latter splendor of this house shall

18. The October 2012 Social Justice Feminism Conference at the University of Cincinnati College of Law is one example of such work, along with the March 2012 "Food and Feminism: Putting the F-Words Together" panel at the Diverse Students' Leadership Conference at Saint Mary's College. The presenters were Susan Alexander, Stacy Davis, Krista Hoefle, Sonalini Sapra, and Bettina Spencer, all Women's Studies appointed or affiliated faculty. See also Heather Laine Talley, "Food is a Feminist Issue," *The Feminist Wire*, 12 July 2011. http://thefeministwire.com/2011/07/food-is-a-feminist-issue. Also, see Nina Power's "Capitalism, Consumerism, and Feminism" *New Left Project*, 25 February 2010, http://www.newleftproject.org/index.php.site/article_comments/capitalism_consumerism_and_feminism.

19. Kessler, *Book of Haggai*, 182.

20. Ibid., 181.

21. Petersen, *Haggai and Zechariah 1–8*, 68.

22. For a short definition of the connection between feminism and binaries, see vivatofu, "binary," *A Feminist Theory Dictionary* (blog), 17 July 2007, http://afeministtheorydictionary.wordpress.com/2007/07/17/binary/.

be greater than the former, says the LORD of hosts; and in this place I will give prosperity [שלום], says the LORD of hosts" (Hag 2:9). Assis and Kessler translate שלום as "peace," a reference to the tranquility the eschaton promises. Meyers and Meyers use "well-being," while Petersen uses "prosperity."[23] שלום contains all of these meanings.[24] God's house and, by extension, God will be glorified and be the source of material and spiritual blessings.

Haggai 2 continues the theme of the first chapter: if the people build the temple and honor God, then God in turn will bless them. The introduction of eschatology, however, is a new development that begins and ends this chapter. John T. Carroll offers a helpful summary of the postexilic phenomenon: "Once disaster had befallen the nation, prophets of the exilic and post-exilic eras awaited God's actions to restore Israel's fortunes."[25] The restoration includes a reversal of fortune that leads to the aggrandizement of the oppressed and their God. The postexilic community, materially poor and politically subjugated in Haggai, will one day be wealthy and powerful, with other nations at its feet.[26] Isaiah 60, another postexilic text, describes the turn of events in even more detail than Hag 2:

> Then you shall see and be radiant; your heart shall thrill and rejoice, because the abundance of the sea shall be brought to you, the wealth of the nations shall come to you. A multitude of camels shall cover you, the young camels of Midian and Ephah; all those from Sheba shall come. They shall bring gold and frankincense, and shall proclaim the praise of the LORD. All the flocks of Kedar shall be gathered to you, the rams of Nebaioth shall minister to you; they shall be acceptable on my altar, and I will glorify my glorious house. . . . The glory of Lebanon shall come to you, the cypress, the plane, and the pine, to beautify the place

23. Assis, "A Disputed Temple," 593; Kessler, *Book of Haggai*, 161; Meyers and Meyers, *Haggai, Zechariah 1–8*, 74; Petersen, *Haggai and Zechariah 1– 8*, 61.

24. BDB 1022–23.

25. John T. Carroll, "Eschatology," in *Eerdmans Dictionary of the Bible*, ed. David Noel Freedman, Allen C. Myers, and Astrid B. Beck (Grand Rapids, MI: Eerdmans 2000), 420.

26. Carole R. Fontaine argues that even women's and children's voices in the Bible reinforce the patriarchal standards of the time. Her words could also be applied here: "The Songs of Miriam, Deborah, Hannah and even that meek and mild Virgin Mary speak glowingly of the vindicating violence of their male god and judge, simply reversing the roles of oppressor and oppressed through divine intervention." Carole R. Fontaine, "The Abusive Bible: On the Use of Feminist Method in Pastoral Contexts," in *A Feminist Companion to Reading the Bible: Approaches, Methods and Strategies*, ed. Athalya Brenner & Carole Fontaine (Sheffield: Sheffield Academic, 1997), 95.

> of my sanctuary; and I will glorify where my feet rest. The descendants of those who oppressed you shall come bending low to you, and all who despised you shall bow down at your feet; they shall call you the City of the Lord, the Zion of the Holy One of Israel. (Isa 60:5-7, 13-14)

To some extent, eschatology offers not only a vision of the future but also a vision of the people's present. What should one say about a people based on their dreams and fantasies?

Of course, desire and hope remain difficult to judge. Any reversal of fortune imagery, real or imagined, has the potential to be problematic. During the Reconstruction period of United States history, southern states consistently made it nearly impossible for freed slaves to own guns, perhaps because they could be used against former slave owners. Southern images of black masculinity came out of that fear of reprisal, with lynching only the most extreme response to it.[27] Historically, no such events happened in postexilic Yehud, but power language, even in the mouths of the subjugated, almost always creates a hierarchy; such a creation should be noted and interrogated. In his positive reading of Hag 2:1-9, Kessler mentions almost in passing that the bringing of the world's wealth to a temple, the acceptance of the temple's particular deity, and the welcoming of international peace "were frequently found both in the imperialist ideology of the ancient Near East, and in various prophetic texts."[28] This seemingly insignificant observation matters a great deal for a feminist reading of the passage. Haggai's glorification of the temple uses language about money, and the cliché that money is power contains an element of truth. Malachi 1 and 3 will drive home this point.

For now, however, a feminist interpretation of Haggai should question the image of a deity that bankrupts other communities for a people's or the deity's sake. The conclusions will say as much about the reader as they do about the God Haggai describes. Utilizing the imperialist eschatology of his context, Haggai prophesies about a powerful God. Such language does not fit comfortably within an egalitarian feminist ideology, suggesting that feminist readers may "need new responses" to the

27. For recent work on southern views of masculinity see Riché Richardson, *Black Masculinity and the U.S. South: From Uncle Tom to Gangsta* (Athens: University of Georgia, 2007) and Craig Thompson Friend and Lorri Glover, *Southern Masculinity: Perspectives on Manhood in the South since Reconstruction* (Athens: University of Georgia, 2004).

28. Kessler, *Book of Haggai*, 192.

questions of eschatology.[29] Carole Fontaine asks, "Are the sentiments expressed [in reversal of fortune passages], however human and understandable, actually sentiments we want to flourish and grow?"[30] What does an ideal future look like for a feminist prophet? The answers will vary, but Haggai's vision may not be one of them.

29. The quotation comes from a line in Ani Difranco's "Brief Bus Stop" on her 1991 Righteous Babe Records release, *Not So Soft*.

30. Fontaine, "The Abusive Bible," 97.

Haggai 2:10-19

Ritual Uncleanness without a Marriage Metaphor

Haggai's third oracle, in early December 520 BCE, begins with the prophet seeking clarification from the priests about holiness and uncleanness. The text uses the priestly ruling to argue that the people, their works, and their offerings are unclean, similar to the state of a person who is defiled by a corpse. Just as that unclean person must be isolated and purified, so must the Israelites be cleansed.

Hebrew Bible prophets do not always have productive working relationships with priests, but Haggai does. For example, in Jer 20:1-2, the priest Pashhur puts Jeremiah "in the stocks" for his prophecies. The priest Amaziah conspires against Amos (7:10-11) and urges him to "go, flee away to the land of Judah" (Amos 7:12). In contrast, Haggai says God instructed him to "ask the priests for a ruling" (2:11), and the priests know it is their job to answer him. When God formed the priesthood, beginning with Aaron and his sons, "The Lord spoke to Aaron" and said, "You are to distinguish between the holy and the common, and between the unclean and the clean; and you are to teach the people of Israel all the statutes that the Lord has spoken to them through Moses" (Lev 10:10-11). By going to the priests, Haggai acknowledges their authority. Although the Temple has not yet been fully restored, the priests can still perform some of their tasks, and Haggai goes to them for assistance at God's request, leaving the priestly leadership role intact.

Hag 2:10-19

10On the twenty-fourth day of the
ninth month, in the second year of
Darius, the word of the LORD came by
the prophet Haggai, saying: 11Thus
says the LORD of hosts: Ask the priests
for a ruling: 12If one carries consecrated
meat in the fold of one's garment, and
with the fold touches bread, or stew, or
wine, or oil, or any kind of food, does
it become holy? The priests answered,
"No." 13Then Haggai said, "If one who
is unclean by contact with a dead body
touches any of these, does it become
unclean?" The priests answered, "Yes,
it becomes unclean." 14Haggai then
said, So it is with this people, and with
this nation before me, says the LORD;
and so with every work of their hands;
and what they offer there is unclean.
15But now, consider what will come to
pass from this day on. Before a stone
was placed upon a stone in the LORD's
temple, 16how did you fare? When one
came to a heap of twenty measures,
there were but ten; when one came to
the wine vat to draw fifty measures,
there were but twenty. 17I struck you
and all the products of your toil with
blight and mildew and hail; yet you did
not return to me, says the LORD. 18Con-
sider from this day on, from the twenty-
fourth day of the ninth month. Since the
day that the foundation of the LORD's
temple was laid, consider: 19Is there
any seed left in the barn? Do the vine,
the fig tree, the pomegranate, and the
olive tree still yield nothing? From this
day on I will bless you.

Haggai, in keeping with the priests' job description, asks specifically about holiness and uncleanness. Can holiness be transmitted to food through the indirect touch of holy meat? The priests say no, holiness can only be directly transmitted, as Lev 6:27-28 suggests. But such holiness is temporary—the blood from consecrated meat must be washed away from clothes and pots, and if the pot cannot be cleaned, then it must be destroyed. Can uncleanness be transmitted to food through indirect touch, for example, when anyone who touches a corpse and is unclean then touches the food? In this case, the priests reply yes, if a person is unclean, then anything that person touches is unclean as well. Numbers 19:11-20 states that contact with a corpse renders a person unclean for seven days. During that time, "a clean person" (Num 19:18) must sprinkle the unclean person and his or her home with water stored especially for this purpose. The priests cite no texts from either Leviticus or Numbers when they answer Haggai's questions, but their short responses are consistent with the Torah's definitions of holiness and uncleanness; as such, the priests have done their job.

Based on the ruling, Haggai states, "So is it with this people, and with this nation before me, says the LORD; and so with every work of their hands; and what they offer there is unclean" (Hag 2:14). The prophetic response suggests that, just as a person who touches a corpse is unclean, along with all that person touches, the postexilic community in Judah is unclean. Further, anything the unclean do in this state is unclean as well; this includes their rebuilding of the temple and "what they offer there," upon some sort of altar.[1] Prophetic claims that the people are unclean are not new; however, the comparison of the people's present state of uncleanness to corpse contamination is new. Previously, when prophets called the people unclean, they often used language that associated uncleanness with femaleness. Israel's apostasy parallels the actions of a sexually unfaithful wife (Jer 2–3; Ezek 16, 23; Hos 1–2). Israel's conduct was like "the uncleanness of a woman in her menstrual period" (Ezek 36:17), which describes immoral behavior. Here, in contrast, Haggai utilizes male imagery. Either masculine singular or plural verbs appear in Hag 2:13-14; also, Numbers 19, which discusses those contaminated by corpses, uses third-person masculine pronouns and verbs. In describing a state of uncleanness, Haggai uses a male simile and not a female simile or metaphor. Impurity in this context lacks an association with women's bodies or actions.

While scholars of Haggai recognize that the prophet makes a declaration of uncleanness, no scholarly consensus exists regarding who or what is unclean. Some argue that the altar being used for sacrifices is unclean and therefore contaminates the sacrifices,[2] or that the temple site itself is the source of uncleanness.[3] Others argue that the people are unclean and are therefore defiling the altar and the sacrifices.[4] Tim Unger insists that Haggai would not call the finally obedient temple builders unclean but questions why the negative perception of them appears in this text, because unclean people by definition do unclean deeds. He concludes

1. Joep Dubbink, "Ähnlich Und Doch Ganz Anders: Priester Und Propheten Über Die Begriffe *Heilig* Und *Unrein*," *Communio Viatorum* 50 (2008): 14–15.

2. Ibid.

3. Ronald J. Sim, "Notes on Haggai 2:10-21," *Journal of Translation and Textlinguistics* 5 (1992): 25–36; Ernst R. Wendland, "Temple Site or Cemetery?—A Question of Perspective," *JOTT* 5, no. 1(1992): 37–85; Paul L. Redditt, *Haggai, Zechariah, Malachi* (Grand Rapids, MI: Eerdmans, 1995), 28; David L. Petersen, *Haggai and Zechariah 1–8: A Commentary* (Philadelphia: Westminster, 1984), 82–84, which argues that both the altar and the temple site are unclean.

4. David R. Hildebrand, "Temple Ritual: A Paradigm for Moral Holiness in Haggai II 10-19," *VT* 39 (1989): 161–64; John Kessler, *The Book of Haggai: Prophecy and Society in Early Persian Yehud* (Leiden: Brill, 2002), 202, 205–6, 215.

that the image is contradictory.[5] The image may be contradictory, but Unger makes a most helpful point: uncleanness refers specifically to actions. Touching a corpse renders a person unclean, and all acts performed in that unclean state become unclean as well. The law does not judge someone's interior life by making a distinction between "ritual holiness [and] ethical holiness," as David Hildebrand suggests.[6] On the contrary, external cleanliness, which will enable someone to enter sacred space, and external holiness, or the doing of good deeds, equals internal holiness. Leviticus 19:2 declares, "You shall be holy, for I the LORD your God am holy." People attain holiness through actions, such as leaving surplus crops behind for the poor, abstaining from lying or cheating, and honoring the aged (Lev 19:9-13, 15, 32, 35-36). Therefore, holiness was within reach. Following the prescribed purification ritual, for example, restores the one who touches a corpse to the community.

Haggai's characterization of the people as unclean, therefore, is not a devastating assessment of their character or moral fiber. The people simply are defiled and need to be cleansed. Unlike earlier woman-centered metaphors of uncleanness, where the contaminated woman either endures rejection (Jeremiah and Hosea) or physical and sexual violation (Ezekiel) as a restoration ritual, Haggai's male-centered image is gentle. Yes, the community suffers from impurity; but just as corpse contamination only requires two baths and some housecleaning to be removed, the unclean community's contamination can be disposed of similarly and easily.

John Kessler observes that "the text does not describe its [the impurity's] source,"[7] but the second half of the oracle suggests that a failure to restore the temple speedily and to purify the building site once the restoration began likely is the source of the uncleanness. Haggai blames poor crop yields on the past delay in temple reconstruction. Because of the people's work "from this day on, from the twenty-fourth day of the ninth month," agricultural success will now be forthcoming (Hag 2:18). On this day, Haggai calls for purification, and the text suggests that a

5. "Diese Uberlegung zeigt, das Haggais Anliegen mit einer Unreinheitsdeklaration, die das eigene Volk trifft, im Widerspruch steht." Tim Unger, "Noch einmal: Haggais unreines Volk," *ZAW* 103 (1991): 220.

6. Hildebrand, "Temple Ritual," 163. Similarly, Carol L. and Eric M. Meyers state, "The absence of what we would, for want of more appropriate language, call the moral dimension of sanctity may explain why it was so difficult to attain sanctity." Meyers and Meyers, *Haggai, Zechariah 1–8, A New Translation with Introduction and Commentary*, AB 25B (New York: Doubleday, 1987), 79.

7. Kessler, *Book of Haggai*, 216.

cleansing ritual takes place that will remove the curse upon the people's produce. Better days now lie ahead.

Haggai first reminds the people of life "before a stone was placed upon a stone in the LORD's temple," and this life was not good (2:15). Grain yields were fifty percent below normal, and wine had decreased by sixty percent. God claims responsibility for the lack of food and drink: "I struck you and all the products of your toil with blight and mildew and hail; yet you did not return to me, says the LORD" (Hag 2:17). As Paul L. Redditt observes, "Haggai, thus, stood in a line of theological reflection that interpreted crop failure and other natural disasters as warnings from God."[8] Interestingly, the word "return" does not appear in the Hebrew text; NRSV translators borrow it from Amos 4:9: "I struck you with blight and mildew; I laid waste your gardens and your vineyards; the locust devoured your fig trees and your olive trees; yet you did not *return* to me, says the LORD" (emphasis mine). Max Rogland, however, points out that even without inserting the word "return," Hag 2:17 still argues that the people initially refuse to support the rebuilding of the temple, which leads to divinely mandated crop failure.[9] These agricultural difficulties are literally, however, old news. Haggai had brought the people's attention to this problem "in the sixth month, on the first day of the month" (1:1), and the people began to rebuild "on the twenty-fourth day of that same month" (1:15). Are crop yields still low? Apparently, the answer is yes; because the people are unclean, blessings continue to be withheld.

Yet "from this day on, from the twenty-fourth day of the ninth month . . . from this day on I will bless you" (Hag 2:18, 19). The day marks "the day that the foundation of the LORD's temple was laid," and this phrase has caused no end of interpretive difficulty (Hag 2:18). If the people began working three months ago, asks Hildebrand, then how can today be a foundation ceremony?[10] Shouldn't life be better today than it was three months ago? Taking the second question first, the answer is no. Haggai informs the people that, their labors notwithstanding, they are unclean. Uncleanness requires purification, so today's foundation ceremony acts as a cleansing ritual that will remove the agricultural blight; to answer the first question, such a ceremony did

8. Redditt, *Haggai, Zechariah, Malachi*, 30.

9. Max Rogland, "Haggai 2, 17 – A New Analysis," *Bib* 88 (2007): 554–56. Therefore, "return" need not mean that Haggai calls the people to repent on this day, as David Hildebrand suggests in "Temple Ritual" (165).

10. Hildebrand, "Temple Ritual," 166.

not have to occur at the beginning of the reconstruction process.[11] Instead, today marks the beginning of the people's purification and the purification of the temple site.

Now, the clean people may anticipate better economic times. Haggai 2:19 asks, "Is there any seed left in the barn? Do the vine, the fig tree, the pomegranate, and the olive tree still yield nothing?" Unlike Haggai's earlier questions to the priests (Hag 2:11-13), Haggai's two questions here receive no direct answer in the text. The people, however, are asked to "consider from this day on" (Hag 2:18), so the implied answers are "no" and "yes." By the time of Haggai's prophecy, the seed for the following year had already been planted.[12] So, the barns may be low at this moment, but "the Lord will certainly bless you with better harvests in the future."[13] Carol L. Meyers and Eric M. Meyers suggest that there was seed in the barn, because blessings came as soon as "work on the temple began" three months earlier: "God is present because the people have dealt with their defilement by responding at last to God's will by agreeing that his house should be restored."[14] The date of Haggai's oracle, however, challenges this reading. If the foundation ceremony is in December, on the same day as Haggai's declaration of the people's uncleanness,[15] then the problem of their defilement could not have been solved back in August or September. Otherwise, no need exists for "the word of the Lord" to come to Haggai now (2:10).

Just as today marks a turning point in grain production, fruit harvests too will improve. Hildebrand notes that "grapes, figs, and pomegranates were harvested in August and September, and olives from September to December. Harvest is in, and there is little to show for it."[16] David J. Clark argues that "it . . . seems unlikely that the two questions would imply opposite answers."[17] If, however, Haggai suggests that from this day, yields will improve,[18] then the answer to the second question will eventually be "yes." According to David Petersen, "Prior to 'this day,'

11. Petersen, *Haggai and Zechariah 1–8*, 88–90; Redditt, *Haggai, Zechariah, Malachi*, 29, 31; Kessler, *Book of Haggai*, 208–09, 216.

12. David J. Clark, "Problems in Haggai 2.15-19," *BT* 34 (1983): 437; Hildebrand, "Temple Ritual," 168; Kessler, *Book of Haggai*, 210.

13. Clark, "Problems in Haggai," 437.

14. Meyers and Meyers, *Haggai, Zechariah 1–8*, 80.

15. Ibid., 82.

16. Hildebrand, "Temple Ritual," 168.

17. Clark, "Problems in Haggai," 438.

18. Ibid., 438–39; Hildebrand, "Temple Ritual," 168; Kessler, *Book of Haggai*, 210.

these particular trees had not borne fruit."[19] Scarcity, however, will soon make way for abundance.

Haggai's oracle makes an argument for divine retribution, but the success of the argument is debatable. The people's initial failure to rebuild the temple and cleanse themselves leads to crop failure. Now that they are obedient, blessings will flow. John Kessler observes that "the crop failures, divine retribution for Temple rebuilding neglect, did not produce the desired repentance. Yahweh's attempts to bring back the community . . . were unfruitful."[20] Nearly two decades before, Petersen makes the same point: these past attacks on grains and fruits did not reform the people's behavior.[21] Just as in Amos 4:9, in Haggai poor harvests do not motivate the people to change their ways; so why does God bother with this punishment? And if the people did not see the connections among their past failure to rebuild the temple, the present need for purification, and their poor harvests, why will they necessarily make a connection between today's cleansing ceremony and future abundant harvests? In Hag 1, the lack of rebuilding causes subpar agricultural production, "yet more than three weeks elapse after Haggai's first oracle before the reconstruction of the temple gets under way."[22] The people may be obedient, but they are not swift. Even after the rebuilding project begins, three months pass before the necessary purification happens. As Petersen states, "Haggai's discourse with the people, his questions and his responses, had moved especially the leaders to action in a way that Yahweh's earlier measures had not moved them."[23] Perhaps, but Haggai is supposed to be "the messenger of the LORD [who] spoke to the people with the LORD's message" (1:13).

The implication is that God had to change tactics because simply smiting the people's produce did not make them rebuild the temple quickly. In order to bring about purification, Haggai acts more like a teacher, leading the people step by step to the desired conclusion, than as a preexilic prophet who loudly proclaims destruction. When the people in Amos do not repent in response to natural disasters, exile is their lot (Amos 4:12-5:7, 5:16-17). By Haggai's time, the exile card already has been played, and the people still do not behave "properly." So, God must develop new ways

19. Petersen, *Haggai and Zechariah 1–8*, 95.
20. Kessler, *Book of Haggai*, 208.
21. Petersen, *Haggai and Zechariah 1–8*, 93.
22. Towner, "Haggai," 1266.
23. Petersen, *Haggai and Zechariah 1–8*, 93.

to make divine arguments clear. The people eventually obey, but God may well have lost some power of persuasion after the exile. Starving the returned exiles into submission no longer works, if it ever did; reasoning with the people, however, achieves the desired result.

The Temple and the Kitchen: Reflections on God as a Hungry Parent in Haggai

Haggai 2:10-19 is a fairly standard prophetic passage in its formula: God, through a prophet (here, Haggai), reminds the people of Israel what they are doing wrong and enumerates the misfortunes that have come their way because of it, and then God explains, succinctly, what needs to be done in order for the people of Israel to turn their misfortunes around.

My preferred method for reading this passage is to attempt to approach it from God's perspective, which renders the otherwise baffling sequence of events familiar. The use of familiar here is quite purposeful: the story becomes familiar in its literal sense. When I try to put myself in the mind of the God that Haggai presents, I feel like a disgruntled parent having a conversation with my disobedient children.

The conversation goes something like this: "Kids, let's review the rules. They are simple rules, right? Here, Joe, why don't you ask your older sister about this one because I'm sure she knows the answer. So Joe, ask Katy whether or not you can eat your dessert if you haven't finished your peas."

Katy responds that, no, neither Joe nor Katy herself can eat the pie that is sitting on the kitchen counter for dessert until they've finished the incredibly small portion of peas sitting on their plates. The response is not news to either of them; as long as both children can remember the rules have been the same. So why does the disgruntled parent have to ask? For the same reason that God sent Haggai to ask the priests a question that would have been more than common knowledge: the seemingly simple, certainly established rule will end up being a metaphor for a larger concept that the children need to understand. In Haggai, the metaphor becomes the uncleanliness of the people themselves, for it seems they have metaphorically (or perhaps literally) been in contact with unclean things. For Katy and Joe, it might be simply that they do not get a treat until they have done what they need to be doing.

Of course, the real issue that Haggai is dealing with is not exactly the degree to which the people of Judah are ritually clean but rather the fact that there is no Temple in which they can become clean once again. The absence of a Temple in Jerusalem during Haggai's time was the source of a great many religious problems, as the Temple was the place of sacrifice and the center of all major ritual practices in ancient Israel. So the particular rule that the Israelites are flaunting in Haggai is a big one: they are practicing religion without a place to practice. Indeed, they are making food without a kitchen.

Let's think back to Joe and Katy for a minute. The kids offer to make their parents sandwiches for dinner. In addition to the very simple rule to wash their hands before preparing food, Katy and Joe are expected to assemble their meal in the kitchen. After all, the kitchen is the room for food preparation. Indeed, it is where food is both prepared and eaten. So when Katy and Joe take the food to their room to prepare it, their poor frustrated parents have to decide whether or not they are going to actually consume this meal that could contain any number of things they do not wish to consume at all.

This metaphor is, of course, imperfect. In order for the metaphor to match more clearly the situation that God is dealing with in Haggai, you must imagine that the kitchen was burned down, perhaps by Joe and Katy's friends. In the actual prophetic story the first Temple is destroyed by the Babylonians, but the actions of the Israelites and their errant religious practices are often cited as the reason the Babylonians were able to come into Jerusalem to destroy it in the first place. So it becomes necessary to imagine that Katy and Joe invited friends over for a party when their parents were gone for the night. Katy and Joe's decision is, perhaps, one of the most egregious rules a child can break. In the course of this breach of the well-established rules, one of the kids at the party becomes over-excited and there is an accident in the kitchen and it is destroyed.

In response, Katy and Joe are grounded for quite some time and are then given the task of fixing the damage in the kitchen. Yes, the task is big; but considering that food is prepared and eaten in the kitchen, it seems obvious why it is so important for the kitchen to be functional once more. The issue of rebuilding the Temple in Haggai is the same situation. Yet in Haggai, from both the people's perspective and God's, the situation is (and certainly should seem) quite a bit more dire—the ancient Israelite religion was primarily a sacrificial cult, and its nucleus was the Temple. Without a Temple, there could not be (or, at least from God's perspective, there should not be) any sacrifices. That means God was not getting the sacrificial sustenance that God requires and was therefore, understandably, unwilling to grant any sort of blessing upon Israel.

Indeed, as this passage describes, the lack of a Temple and the delay in having it built following the return of some of the exiled Judeans to Jerusalem is so disturbing to God that there is not only a lack of blessing but the imposition of punishment. Verse 17 sounds like a clear parental plea to children who continue to refuse to do what is expected of them. God says, "Look, kids, you didn't do what you were supposed to do so I had to punish you. And somehow, even after I gave you what you deserved, you still haven't done the very critical and extremely important thing I asked you to do." Granted, God's form of punishment is to essentially destroy the crops and bring about natural disasters, but in its way it is not entirely dissimilar to a good grounding or parent-enforced prohibition from the phone or internet.

Like all good parents, however, God does not ever seem to give up on the wayward child that is Israel. The passage ends with God assuring Israel that, as soon as the foundation for the new Temple is laid, the punishment will end and it will be replaced with blessing (verse 19). It is like Joe and Katy's parents telling them that, when the kitchen is repaired, not only will their grounding be over but they will get to go on a trip to the zoo or their favorite amusement park. It is a fitting end to a frustrating story and a familiar ending to a far too common parent-child cycle of interaction. At the end of the day, the message is simple: make sure God is fed, and please try to remember that there are some very basic rules of living that need to be followed. Once you've got that covered, all will be well, at least in the Haggai narrative.

Rebecca M. Jones

Haggai 2:20-23

The Personal as Political as Theological

Now that Haggai has persuaded the people to rebuild the temple and return to God's good graces, he receives a final message for Zerubbabel's ears only. Haggai 2:21-23 repeats and intensifies the violent eschatological imagery of Hag 2:6-7, while including God's glorification of Zerubbabel. Although he does not appear to be a messiah because God takes the active role in Haggai's eschatological scenario, Zerubbabel's exaltation remains significant. He stands both as a political and a theological figure—God will reward and restore the humble and obedient, even if their social context turns out to be less than ideal.

On the same day as his prophecy about cleanliness and prosperity, Haggai speaks directly "to Zerubbabel, governor of Judah" (2:20). The message from God reiterates the shaking theme from two months ago,[1] with more negative consequences for the nations: God says, "I am about to shake the heavens and the earth, and to overthrow the throne of kingdoms; I am about to destroy the strength of the kingdoms of the nations,

1. Paul L. Redditt, *Haggai, Zechariah, Malachi* (Grand Rapids, MI: Eerdmans, 1995), 31; John Kessler, *The Book of Haggai: Prophecy and Society in Early Persian Yehud* (Leiden: Brill, 2002), 227.

Hag 2:20-23

[20]The word of the LORD came a second time to Haggai on the twenty-fourth day of the month: [21]Speak to Zerubbabel, governor of Judah, saying, I am about to shake the heavens and the earth, [22]and to overthrow the throne of kingdoms; I am about to destroy the strength of the kingdoms of the nations, and overthrow the chariots and their riders; and the horses and their riders shall fall, every one by the sword of a comrade. [23]On that day, says the LORD of hosts, I will take you, O Zerubbabel my servant, son of Shealtiel, says the LORD, and make you like a signet ring; for I have chosen you, says the LORD of hosts.

and overthrow the chariots and their riders; and the horses and their riders shall fall, every one by the sword of a comrade" (Hag 2:21-22). Earlier in the chapter, the eschatological "message focused primarily on the economic implications of that threat"; this message, however, is political.[2] John Kessler notes that God will destroy the nations by facilitating a world war. He further observes that "the shaking of the cosmos . . . is frequently found in eschatological descriptions. As well, the mutual destruction of armies in panic is a common element."[3] The description bears not only "fundamental military connotations" but also political relevance.[4] Carol L. and Eric M. Meyers state that Hag 2:22 "anticipates the end of any foreign domination, no matter how benign or minimal, over Yehud."[5] Both in ancient and in modern times, a nation's strength is frequently seen as its military might. If all armies fall, then Yehud and its people, although lacking an independent army, no longer reside at the bottom of the world's hierarchy. God eliminates the hierarchy altogether by enabling all other armies to kill each other off.

In the middle of the bloodshed, where will Zerubbabel be, since this prophecy is directed to him? God calls Zerubbabel "my servant," making Zerubbabel, the recipient of divine favor and selection, "like a signet ring" (Hag 2:23). The verse's imagery has generated a significant amount of discussion. At minimum, Zerubbabel appears "as *an image of Yahweh's*

2. Redditt, *Haggai, Zechariah, Malachi*, 31, 32.

3. Kessler, *Book of Haggai*, 224, 225.

4. David L. Petersen, *Haggai and Zechariah 1–8: A Commentary* (Philadelphia: Westminster, 1984), 102.

5. Carol L. Meyers and Eric M. Meyers, *Haggai, Zechariah 1–8, A New Translation with Introduction and Commentary*, AB 25B (New York: Doubleday, 1987), 67.

favour . . . and the manifestation of that favour in the experience of the individual addressed."[6] Whether this image is royal or messianic, however, depends on which scholar one reads. Paul L. Redditt argues that Haggai envisions Zerubbabel as the reinstated Davidic king of Judah.[7] Janet E. Tollington concurs; for her, "it appears probable that Haggai envisaged imminent eschatological activity by Yahweh which would result in political independence for the community in Jerusalem and necessitate there being a political leader, and that Zerubbabel would be that leader appointed by Yahweh."[8] John Kessler is more cautious, suggesting that Zerubbabel's glorification, while perhaps royal, need not be.[9] No "explicitly royal language appears," and the text does not mention "Zerubbabel's supremacy over the nations."[10] David L. Petersen notes that Hag 2:23 may sound royal, but the language also sounds vague and neither clearly political nor pointedly messianic.[11] Meyers and Meyers state that Zerubbabel is not "a messianic figure"; instead, he acts as "a participant in God's administration of the nations of the world but not the initiator or leader in that task."[12]

The Harper Collins Study Bible's subtitle for Hag 2:20-23 reads "God's Promise to Zerubbabel," but the arguments against Zerubbabel as a royal or messianic figure are more persuasive because of God's role in the text. Even the pro-messiah arguments note that God and not Zerubbabel remains the star of the eschatological show. Redditt states that Zerubbabel will be under God's authority, and for Tollington, any power that Zerubbabel receives will come from God's action and not his own effort.[13] While any king or messiah would be subservient to God, Zerubbabel's complete lack of activity in the passage is significant. He is not only subservient but also inert. Meyers and Meyers conclude as follows: "The two words, 'servant' and 'signet,' with which Haggai characterizes Zerubbabel's role are both terms of instrumentality and hence do not suggest direct monarchic powers."[14] God, not a human ruler, overthrows

6. Kessler, *Book of Haggai*, 231 (italics in original).

7. Redditt, *Haggai, Zechariah, Malachi*, 32.

8. Janet E. Tollington, *Tradition and Innovation in Haggai and Zechariah 1–8* (Sheffield: JSOT Press, 1993), 143–44.

9. Kessler, *Book of Haggai*, 235–38, 240.

10. Ibid., 237, 240.

11. Petersen, *Haggai and Zechariah 1–8*, 104–5.

12. Meyers and Meyers, *Haggai, Zechariah 1–8*, 83.

13. Redditt, *Haggai, Zechariah, Malachi*, 32; Tollington, *Tradition and Innovation*, 136.

14. Meyers and Meyers, *Haggai, Zechariah 1–8*, 68.

the nations. The prophecy therefore emphasizes God's leadership and sovereignty. God stirs up the people to rebuild the temple and brings down all other nations, either acting directly or orchestrating human activity. Zerubbabel may be God's servant, just as Cyrus of Persia was God's anointed as the one who ended the exile in Second Isaiah (Isa 40–55), but God remains in charge. As Second Isaiah states, "I am the Lord, and there is no other. I form light and create darkness. I make weal and create woe; I the Lord do all these things" (45:6-7). Haggai himself, while successful, depends on "the word of the Lord" for that success (1:1, 2:1, 2:10, and 2:20). Greg Goswell rejects a messianic interpretation of Hag 2:20-23, because "the overall temple-focus of Haggai's eschatology, what the temple symbolizes (God's palace) and anticipates (the universal reign of God), makes it unlikely that 2:20-23 promotes messianism."[15] The rejection of messianism or royalty makes sense in light of the book's focus on restoring not only the temple but also the status of the one who lives there (Hag 1:8 and 2:8).

If Zerubbabel is neither king nor messiah, then why does God choose him and for what purpose? Kessler warns against speculation: "The precise moment of Yahweh's choice, and its basis, are not explicitly stated. . . . The text is quite discreet regarding these matters, and dogmatism is ill-advised."[16] After all, the idea of arbitrary divine selection reappears in postexilic prophecy with Mal 1:3—God says, "Yet I have loved Jacob but I have hated Esau." Yet, because Kessler compares Zerubbabel's creation "like a signet ring" to Jehoiachin's guaranteed rejection, "even if [he] were the signet ring on [God's] right hand" (Jer 22:24), speculation here becomes difficult to resist.[17] According to 2 Kgs 24:9, Jehoiachin was rejected because he "did what was evil in the sight of the Lord, just as his father had done." While this may not be the strongest of explanations, it argues against complete arbitrariness. Goswell suggests that "due to the valuable service that Zerubbabel as governor has rendered the temple-building program . . . he is promised God's protection."[18] Kessler also entertains this possibility.[19] With Haggai prophesying mass destruction of the strong and powerful, at least

15. Greg Goswell, "The Fate and Future of Zerubbabel in the Prophecy of Haggai," *Bib* 91 (2010), 84.

16. Ibid., 84.

17. Ibid., 226, 231.

18. Ibid., 89.

19. Kessler, *Book of Haggai*, 233 n. 87.

Zerubbabel, a seemingly lowly provincial governor, will be safe. His obedience to God receives a just reward.

God chooses Zerubbabel, but Haggai gives no word on the status of the other Israelites and non-Israelite peoples. Zerubbabel has not been building the temple alone. Also, foreign armies will fall, but what about the rest of the nations? Haggai falls silent here, but placing his second eschatological prophecy in conversation with his first one suggests that whoever survives among the nations will be poor and powerless. While the new temple will overflow with wealth, there is no indication that the Israelites themselves will be either wealthy or world leaders. The only one who benefits from the divinely instigated changes is God. Haggai 2:7 does not create a new human hierarchy but a type of theocracy.[20] All mortals are in a humble state, with God at the head. Zephaniah, a preexilic prophetic work, describes the purge of the wicked on "the day of the LORD " in chapters 1 and 2. But chapter 3 sketches a more peaceful scene that will follow the purging: "At that time I will change the speech of the peoples to a pure speech, that all of them may call on the name of the LORD and serve him with one accord. From beyond the rivers of Ethiopia my suppliants, my scattered ones, shall bring my offering" (Zeph 3:9-10). In Zephaniah's eschaton, the surviving Gentiles become God's servants, but not the Israelites' slaves. Instead, "I will leave in the midst of you a people humble and lowly. They shall seek refuge in the name of the LORD—the remnant of Israel" (Zeph 3:12-13).

So far, no eschatological vision offers an egalitarian ideal. The only question is who will be in charge, and the answer is God. A modest world community without military might does little internal harm and poses no external threat to God. Just as in the Tower of Babel story, when God creates different languages as a check on human power (Gen 11:5-7), the eschaton will serve the same purpose of restraining humankind and expanding God's dominion.[21]

20. Unlike in Isaiah 23, where the people receive the benefits of God's possibly forced prostitution of Tyre, the plundered wealth in Haggai 2 goes directly to God and appears to stay there.

21. According to Adele Reinhartz: "The dispersion and confusion of languages was HaShem's way of creating obstacles for large-scale co-operative projects and circumventing a potential threat to divine hegemony, power and authority" ("Feminist Criticism and Biblical Studies on the Verge of the Twenty-First Century," in *A Feminist Companion to Reading the Bible: Approaches, Methods and Strategies*, ed. Athalya Brenner and Carole Fontaine [Sheffield: Sheffield Academic, 1997], 36).

The comments on Hag 2:1-9 reveal a discomfort with eschatology that Hag 2:20-23 has not eliminated, even with the Zephaniah comparison. Yet examining Haggai's final prophecy from a post-colonial perspective expands its range of meanings. Steed Vernyl Davidson's notes on Haggai in *The Peoples' Bible* are instructive here. As a native of Trinidad and Tobago, Davidson sees similarities between his own country's post-colonial development and Haggai's context. Regarding Hag 2:20-23, Davidson recognizes the hopes that the community may have pinned upon Zerubbabel, specifically "the promise of a restored monarchy (2:23). These aspirations reflect the desire of colonized peoples not only to have their own leaders but to have leaders that mirror their indigenous needs and culture."[22] Zerubbabel, however, does not become just another symbol of human imperialism. Davidson concludes,

> Yet on that day, Zerubbabel plays no role, but merely stands by as a spectator of God's power. The centrality of the temple does not assume a central leader that accumulates power to himself . . . This vision offers a trans-historical perspective that shows a time when even the imperial powers will no longer exist. The prophet's message to the community in Jerusalem during the reign of Darius encouraged the rebuilding of the temple—the symbol of the presence of God and of the power of God in the face of empire, and a vision that outlasts temporal powers.[23]

God's power may destroy the nations, but that destruction gives the poor and oppressed people a chance to "pasture and lie down, and no one shall make them afraid" (Zeph 3:13). War creates (hopefully) lasting peace, with God as the designer of both.

Some commentaries about Haggai conclude with an overall assessment of the prophet's work. Redditt states that "the book of Haggai seems to have been too optimistic."[24] The temple does not become the center of the ancient Near East, and Zerubbabel quickly disappears from history. According to Meyers and Meyers, "That his prophecy was not fulfilled historically only serves to confirm its authenticity"; they point out that, eschatological visions notwithstanding, Haggai succeeds because the

22. Steed Verynl Davidson, "Haggai," in *The Peoples' Bible*, ed. Curtiss Paul DeYoung, Wilda C. Gafney, Leticia A. Guardiola-Sáenz, George "Tink" Tinker, and Frank M. Yamada (Minneapolis: Fortress, 2008), 1098.

23. Ibid., 1096.

24. Redditt, *Haggai, Zechariah, Malachi*, 34.

temple is restored.[25] And the book itself remains as a symbol of hope. Haggai's eschatology acknowledges the Israelites' political subjugation but also includes hope for a better future, or what Kessler calls a "theological compromise."[26] In Haggai's historical context, he does accomplish his objective, the reconstruction of the temple. Through reasoning, cheerleading, and promises of future prosperity, work on the temple takes place. Years later, the book of Ezra credits Haggai for his assistance with the temple project (5:1-2). His postexilic status is secure.

The call for the reconstruction of the temple takes place during the reign of Darius I. Jon L. Berquist states that Darius' political agenda was "the creation of a formalized bureaucratic structure" that ensured loyalty to the empire and a steady flow of taxes; Zerubbabel and Haggai were political and rhetorical means to that end.[27] If the call to rebuild comes out of a Persian and not an Israelite agenda, then it sounds less like a call for religious revival and more like a call for political survival. Petersen argues that Haggai's description of Zerubbabel must be vague precisely because Zerubbabel governs a Persian province.[28] Talk of an independent leader would bring the might of Persia down on the people's heads. Having just been freed from Babylon, destroyers of the first temple, no one in Yehud wanted a repeat of that experience. Yet if Haggai prophesies as a Persian pawn,[29] then his words are even more remarkable because he successfully convinces the people to do something that will not necessarily benefit them. Berquist concludes, "It is reasonable to assume that the residents of Yehud understood that the temple would benefit others, such as the Persian Empire and the priests appointed by Darius, more than it would advantage the workers."[30] To transform an earthly demand into a divine request and de-emphasize the political implications of that demand is no small accomplishment.

Even if the temple itself functions as a historical and political symbol of Persian domination, it also functions as a symbol of life. Existence in Yehud may be challenging, as Malachi will reiterate, and political

25. Meyers and Meyers, *Haggai, Zechariah 1–8*, 84, 87.

26. Kessler, *Book of Haggai*, 241, 242.

27. Jon L. Berquist, *Judaism in Persia's Shadow: A Social and Historical Approach* (Minneapolis: Fortress, 1995), 61.

28. Petersen, *Haggai and Zechariah 1–8*, 106.

29. Berquist, *Judaism in Persia's Shadow*, 65, 67.

30. Ibid., 70. This understanding may explain the people's lack of interest in supporting the temple, about which Malachi complains vigorously in chapters one and three.

freedom may be only a dream, but the dead cannot dream at all. Survival as a subjugated people is not ideal but perhaps is its own small good. Second-wave feminists insisted that the personal is political. For Haggai, the political is theological. Even if the prophet uses the language and imagery of imperialism, he does so for the sake of keeping the postexilic community together. Framing a political act (rebuilding the temple) as a religious one reminds the laborers of their past and present identity as God's people and not only of their status as Persian subjects. The use of "Zerubbabel, son of Shealtiel, governor of Judah" (Hag 1:1, 2:2) and "Zerubbabel, governor of Judah" (Hag 2:21) may serve the same purpose. Haggai does not remind the people that they live in Yehud, Persia's province. They live in Judah, what the land was called before the exile and subsequent conquests. Naming is its own form of power, and not using the provincial name is its own form of resistance, however subtle. To rebuild the temple is a sign of life. Haggai's words become the sign of that same purpose for his audience at that time and remain a sign today of what living as a conquered people may look like.

Malachi 1:1-5

God Is Love?

Unlike Haggai, which opens with specific identification of person and date, Malachi begins ambiguously: "An oracle. The word of the LORD to Israel by Malachi" (1:1). The words of Nahum and Habakkuk also are called oracles, but Nahum refers specifically to Nineveh, and Habakkuk speaks as a prophet. Malachi's oracle identifies no subject and does not designate the speaker as a prophet. Malachi may not even be a proper name.[1] The unclear beginning warns of uncertainties to come. Each of the following oracles may be more appropriately called complaints. The people (usually identified as "you") challenge God's goodness and honor, which God, like a beleaguered parent of a teenager, tries to defend.

In the first oracle, God speaks in a placating tone, claiming that his favoritism toward Jacob and rejection of Esau proves his love. Such proof, however, confirms the current instability of the divine-human relationship. If a parent loves and hates children arbitrarily, then how secure can any child feel? Also, the proof of love consists solely of a description of

1. Jon L. Berquist, *Judaism in Persia's Shadow: A Social and Historical Approach* (Minneapolis: Fortress, 1995), 94; W. Sibley Towner, "Haggai," in *The Harper Collins Study Bible, Fully Revised and Updated*, ed. Harold W. Attridge (San Francisco: HarperSanFrancisco, 2006), 1284.

Mal 1:1-5

[1]An oracle. The word of the LORD to Israel by Malachi. [2]I have loved you, says the LORD. But you say, "How have you loved us?" Is not Esau Jacob's brother? says the LORD. Yet I have loved Jacob [3]but I have hated Esau; I have made his hill country a desolation and his heritage a desert for jackals. [4]If Edom says, "We are shattered but we will rebuild the ruins," the LORD of hosts says: They may build, but I will tear down, until they are called the wicked country, the people with whom the LORD is angry forever. [5]Your own eyes shall see this, and you shall say, "Great is the LORD beyond the borders of Israel!"

destroying the hated child, suggesting that nurture is not this parent's strong suit.

The people ask God plainly, "How have you loved us?" (Mal 1:2). The text gives no context for the question, only suggesting that the people feel unloved. One justification for the people's feelings may appear in the second and fifth oracles, when God accuses priests and laity of cheating and theft (Mal 1:14, 3:8). Similar to Haggai, the community seems to claim financial hardship and holds back its limited resources. The actions may be a response to a reduction in assistance from Persia, which was spending large amounts of money on military expeditions.[2] Haggai's vision of economic prosperity after the temple's reconstruction has not materialized. Consequently, God appears not to have acted in a loving way toward Israel.

God, however, insists that divine hatred of Esau demonstrates divine love for Jacob. According to Mal 1:2-4, "I have loved Jacob but I have hated Esau; I have made his hill country a desolation and his heritage a desert for jackals. If Edom says, 'We are shattered but we will rebuild the ruins,' the LORD of hosts says: They may build, but I will tear down, until they are called the wicked country, the people with whom the LORD is angry forever." Since other biblical texts, including Obadiah's vision, call for Edom's destruction, Malachi's claim that God loves Jacob by hating Esau seems to make sense. God specifically chose Jacob over Esau, the future Israel over Edom.[3] John D. W. Watts argues that Malachi's

2. Berquist, *Judaism in Persia's Shadow*, 89–93.

3. Paul L. Redditt, *Haggai, Zechariah, Malachi* (Grand Rapids, MI: Eerdmans, 1995), 162; David L. Petersen, *Zechariah 9–14 and Malachi: A Commentary* (Louisville, KY: Westminster John Knox, 1995), 173; Karl William Weyde, *Prophecy and Teaching: Prophetic Authority, Form Problems, and the Use of Traditions in the Book of Malachi* (Berlin: Walter de Gruyter, 2000), 173.

theme is "the love of God for Israel," and this love is "wonderful and improbable."[4] The people's uncertainty about divine justice finds a resolution in the knowledge that, though Judah suffers, Edom suffers more; therefore God loves them and not Edom.[5]

But does the claim make sense? David L. Petersen calls the passage "peculiar," and Paul L. Redditt concludes, "It is not immediately clear that even such a confession [God hates Esau] would prove the prophet's point that God 'loved' Jacob, though it clearly shows that he 'hated' Esau."[6] The idea that love can be shown through unloving actions, however, has biblical precedent. Psalm 137 calls on someone to avenge Israel against Babylon by slaughtering the city's infants, but it also calls on God to "remember . . . against the Edomites, the day of Jerusalem's fall, how they said, 'Tear it down! Tear it down! Down to its foundations!' " (137:7). The psalmist describes singers, possibly those men who once sang within the temple, who refuse to entertain their captors with "songs of Zion" (137:3-4). For the exiles, love means destruction of the beloved's enemy: "Happy shall they shall be who take your little ones and dash them against the rock!" (137:9). For patriarchal people in a limited goods society, it makes sense that there is only so much love to go around.[7] The Genesis story to which Mal 1:2-5 indirectly refers makes this point. Since God loves Jacob, there will inevitably be little to no love for Esau. Once Isaac blesses Jacob, tradition and the limits of real estate dictate that he has no blessing left for Esau (Gen 27:35-50). Fathers can and do play favorites.[8]

This intertextual reading aside, no intratextual reason exists for God's love for one people and rejection of another, unless one considers Mal 1:5. The oracle's concluding verse states, "Your own eyes shall see this [Edom's destruction] and you shall say, 'Great is the LORD beyond the borders of Israel!' " God's actions should lead to honor from the people, a primary objective in the ancient world. Written in the same century as Malachi, Euripides's *Bacchae* narrates the brutal demise of Thebes, a city that rejects

4. John D.W. Watts, "A Frame for the Book of the Twelve: Hosea 1–3 and Malachi," in *Reading and Hearing the Book of the Twelve*, eds. James D. Nogalski and Marvin A. Sweeney (Atlanta, GA: SBL, 2000), 210, 214.

5. Arndt Meinhold, "Gottesungewissheit: Zum Vernhältnis von Form und Inhalt in Mal 1,2–5," *CV* 39 (1997): 149–50.

6. Petersen, *Zechariah 9—14 and Malachi*, 169; Redditt, *Haggai, Zechariah, Malachi*, 161.

7. Bruce J. Malina, *The New Testament World: Insights from Cultural Anthropology*, rev. ed. (Louisville, KY: Westminster John Knox, 1993), 95–96.

8. Redditt, *Haggai, Zechariah, Malachi*, 163.

Dionysus's divinity. When two of the characters protest at the play's end, Dionysus responds twice that he has been blasphemed.[9] Treated dishonorably and disrespectfully, Dionysus may do whatever is necessary to restore his reputation, even if it means destroying those in his path for his own glorification. While theoretically God merits honor simply by virtue of being a deity, apparently even deities must earn respect.

Defense of divine honor extends beyond prize-winning Greek tragedy. God destroys Edom in Ezek 35, and, if they rebuild, their repeated destruction will cause the Edomites and everyone else to "know that I am the LORD" (35:9, 15). But even God's blessing and redemption of Israel takes place for God's aggrandizement and not Israel's benefit, according to Ezek 36: "Therefore say to the house of Israel, Thus says the LORD God: It is not for your sake, O house of Israel, that I am about to act, but for the sake of my holy name, which you have profaned among the nations to which you came. . . . It is not for your sake that I will act, says the LORD GOD; let that be known to you" (36:22, 32). God behaves as a superhero, but one whose primary objective is to save himself and not anyone else. When the people question God's ability to act in Malachi, God responds with a promise of future action, just as in Ezekiel, and claims to be the almighty paterfamilias, powerful, manly, "the Man."

The back-and-forth style of Malachi, however, suggests a tarnishing of God's manly image. If the people wholeheartedly believe in God's love and greatness, then why do the next six oracles indicate human disregard for divine commands and divine complaint about human disrespect? The retributive and hierarchical relationship between God and Israel that dominates so much of the Hebrew Bible has broken down again, and the people do not care. Instead of a book dominated by verses and verses of "obey or else," Malachi's author includes verses of the people's bad acts, bad attitudes, and bad words. Simply put, the people as Malachi characterizes them are not impressed. Surprisingly, Edom's treatment may exacerbate their lack of enthusiasm. Petersen calls "the action and attitude of Yahweh toward Edom [a] violation of a covenant with Edom and invocation of curses"; God takes back land promised in Deut 2:4-5.[10] The accusation of covenant violation appears frequently in Malachi, but not just in God's mouth. If God can break one promise in an attempt to make

9. Euripides, *The Bacchae*, trans. William Arrowsmith, in *Euripides V: Electra, The Phoenician Women, The Bacchae*, ed. David Grene and Richmond Lattimore (Chicago: University of Chicago Press, 1968), 218–19.

10. Petersen, *Zechariah 9–14 and Malachi*, 170.

Israel feel better, then why not break another to pacify someone else? Underneath questions about God's love lie questions about God's faithfulness, power, and carefully constructed masculinity.

Yes, fine, but why do I [Esau] get dragged into this?— A disparaged Scriptural sibling speaks up!

Let me be direct, but even then, while carrying the torch of truthfulness, I'm not so sure my voice will carry much else, certainly not credibility. Is this self-pity? Sour apples? Not really. However, I am well acquainted with how traditional and copious interpretations transmit my tale. The prophet Malachi is enlisted as yet another tale-bearer of Esau's ethical emptiness. The history held onto by much of your civilization casts my tale into a mindset that leaves me little maneuvering room. If I defend myself, I am guilty in your eyes; if I do not lift up my voice in self-protection, I betray myself. What a rotten place for a guy to be, especially one whose Grandfather, Father, and Brother are Patriarchs!

Despite how I see my years, your perspectives proscribe my autonomy. Here we are in Malachi, a long step and lengthy stroll from the fields of Genesis where I began to learn about being a least-beloved sibling. Now, I'm to comment on an array of passages that draw me as somewhat of a fall-guy, positioning "nasty Esau's" reputation as a way not to be, a path to avoid, instructions to discard. I am invited to the party as a poor example. This can happen when people play with the Bible without proper intention; do not forget—to enlist as audience to Biblical lore is to take side and part in a large family's generational gerrymandering.

This is what is done by many who build a Tradition, any Tradition, not only the one which each reader claims as her collective. This is the loyalty which often sustains many denominations years after their utility expires. It is about sociology, religious sociology mind you, but sociology nonetheless. We may come to see how this sociology is less morally troublesome than it is universally practiced.

So, while comprehending this fact on a broader scale, I still cannot help raise a question. Is my disparagement a foot-stool for my extended Israelite family members who are shown and seen in a kinder Scriptural light? Am I truly expected to endure that display, let alone embrace it? If so, try this advice in your own family's unfoldings. I ponder how generous of heart you will be.

Malachi-The-Official-Story opens with God, God's Very Self, Creation's Source and Personification, Who is found using me and my lineage as the means of a curse. The implications of the very opening are hardly benign. The burden of the word of the Lord to Israel by Malachi. . . . (now drop down just a bit and you'll read) Was not Esau Jacob's brother, . . . but Esau I hated.

"Burden"—go ahead, start a conversation with such a Divinely Sanctioned implication. God's burden is found in your tribe's telling! My mountains are made "desolate." My heritage is assigned to "the jackals of the wilderness." My reputation is dumped into a Biblical bargain-basement of scraps and rejects, ill-matched intrigues from a larger tale that prove awkward or inconvenient, shoved aside away from the light of day for the ugliness they either contain or imply.

We are a mere five verses into Malachi. My angst is about more than "Esau rescuing his ego from another's retelling." This musing also concerns the souls of those who claim to own and tell any Esau's story. Be cautious. We deal with Scripture. What is inflicted in one generation is felt decades if not centuries later. Your readings cover blessings and curses. Do not be naive!

I recognize your age is alert to the compelling force of narrative and nurture called "political correctness." You believe you observe the realities of your epoch. You believe you sincerely understand imperatives transmitted. You honestly believe yourselves fully sensitive to those outcast. You are not the first to firmly and righteously believe that your priorities accrue merit.

Sincerity without authenticity does not make for merit. Merit, this side of Eternity, is rarely unearned. You make assumptions when you do not question your own quotas. It is idolatry, a trait my kin often carry-as-accusation, when your precious assumptions go unchallenged, protected all the more so when the ground you occupy to pursue Truth is that of religion, faith, and Scripture. Fortunately, it is those like me, Esau, that come to disturb such arrogance, such tranquility. Complacency and religiosity combine to beg for upheaval. Is this my purpose? Your reply is part of the traditional telling too! Answer well.

I do not petition Jewish-Christian Scriptures to betray their own intentions; I acknowledge that, even though I may be excluded in many ways, there is a great covenant to be affirmed and enacted. I will find ways to craft a constituency outside the bounds and incomplete blessings of your reckonings. Those who are seen as tangential throughout time immemorial manage to go on though their persistence and presence was afforded little significance. My goal need not stem from your expulsion but from my prerogatives. I shall find a territory off the maps that chart your world.

My point and place in this legacy may be redemptive precisely due to my exclusion. Knowing where to put me may tell the reader his own place in the Biblical legacy. Making sense of characters like me forces those who remain within a tradition to solidify or adjust their posture. Where my story is heard and honored, it is hard for arrogance and restrictive ethnicity to gel. I suffer for how the diminishment of one appears necessary to establish another. I dissent when the deprecation of this one seems essential to embellish that one. Is such rivalry without option? Is it a ruse crowned by fears we foist on each other? Can the narratives we see as our justification condemn others and equally belittle ourselves? Does the litany of my questions permit much liberality in response? Perhaps these quandaries dispense with any anxiety over my perceived unpleasantness in these Scriptural presentations. The Esau you know can withstand the uncertainty. Can you?

Rabbi Steven Leapman

Malachi 1:6–2:9

Divine Masculinity Under Attack

Malachi 1:6–2:9 makes up the longest oracle in a short book. The text presents a divine complaint against priestly acceptance of substandard sacrificial animals. By offering these sacrifices, the priests violate a covenant between themselves and God. Several sections within the oracle stand out: God's insistence upon his reputation in Mal 1:11 and 14; the question of whether God finds fault with priests and/or Levites in Mal 2:1-9; and, the description of a heretofore little-known priestly covenant in Mal 2:4-7. The idea of power, however, holds these sections together. God insists that as a "father," "master," and "great King" (Mal 1:6, 14) he deserves proper respect. Not only does such respect fail to materialize, but the priests also show no interest in changing their ways. Similar to Haggai, God argues his case before an apathetic audience. The priestly class depends on the sacrificial system for survival, and the willingness to accept any sacrifice, however "inferior," indicates a conscious privileging of human needs (food) over an abstract ideal (divine glory). Those bringing the defective animals act as the silent partner in the God-priest relationship. Upon them rests the entire temple structure, and therefore they may have the most power of all. They offer what they see fit, without consequences besides divine criticism and feigned priestly ignorance.

The oracle starts by describing a seemingly unbalanced relationship between God and the priests. Karl W. Weyde calls the beginning of Mal

Mal 1:6–2:9

6 A son honors his father, and ser-
vants their master. If then I am a father,
where is the honor due me? And if I am
a master, where is the respect due me?
says the LORD of hosts to you, O priests,
who despise my name. You say, "How
have we despised your name?" 7 By of-
fering polluted food on my altar. And
you say, "How have we polluted it?" By
thinking that the LORD's table may be
despised. 8 When you offer blind ani-
mals in sacrifice, is that not wrong? And
when you offer those that are lame or
sick, is that not wrong? Try presenting
that to your governor; will he be pleased
with you or show you favor? says the
LORD of hosts. 9 And now implore the
favor of God, that he may be gracious
to us. The fault is yours. Will he show
favor to any of you? says the LORD of
hosts. 10 Oh, that someone among you
would shut the temple doors, so that
you would not kindle fire on my altar in
vain! I have no pleasure in you, says
the LORD of hosts, and I will not accept
an offering from your hands. 11 For from
the rising of the sun to its setting my
name is great among the nations, and
in every place incense is offered to my
name, and a pure offering; for my name
is great among the nations, says the
LORD of hosts. 12 But you profane it when
you say that the LORD's table is polluted,
and the food for it may be despised.
13 "What a weariness this is," you say,
and you sniff at me, says the LORD of
hosts. You bring what has been taken
by violence or is lame or sick, and this
you bring as your offering! Shall I ac-
cept that from your hand? says the

1:6 ("A son honors his father, and servants their master") a proverb.[1] At minimum, the sentence expresses the expectations of fathers and masters, which in God's case are unmet. Malachi 1:6 continues as follows: "If then I am a father, where is the honor due me? And if I am a master, where is the respect due me? says the LORD of hosts to you, O priests, who despise my name." Weyde notes, "Perhaps the possibility should also be considered that the two rhetorical questions in Mal 1:6 contain a *complaint*; YHWH complains to the priests that he is not honoured or feared."[2] The possibility finds support in light of the next set of questions, which the text places in the priests' mouths. Claiming not to recognize their troublesome behavior, God says they ask how they have disrespected God and the altar (Mal 1:6-7).

The answer to both questions literally lies on the altar in the form of blind, lame, and sick animals (Mal 1:8). The priests accept these animals,

1. Karl William Weyde, *Prophecy and Teaching: Prophetic Authority, Form Problems, and the Use of Traditions in the Book of Malachi* (Berlin: de Gruyter, 2000), 116.

2. Ibid.

LORD. 14 Cursed be the cheat who has a
male in the flock and vows to give it,
and yet sacrifices to the LORD what is
blemished; for I am a great King, says
the LORD of hosts, and my name is rev-
erenced among the nations.

2:1 And now, O priests, this com-
mand is for you. 2 If you will not listen,
if you will not lay it to heart to give glory
to my name, says the LORD of hosts,
then I will send the curse on you and I
will curse your blessings; indeed I have
already cursed them, because you do
not lay it to heart. 3 I will rebuke your
offspring, and spread dung on your
faces, the dung of your offerings, and
I will put you out of my presence.

4 Know, then, that I have sent this
command to you, that my covenant with
Levi may hold, says the LORD of hosts.
5 My covenant with him was a covenant
of life and well-being, which I gave him;
this called for reverence, and he re-
vered me and stood in awe of my
name. 6 True instruction was in his
mouth, and no wrong was found on his
lips. He walked with me in integrity and
uprightness, and he turned many from
iniquity. 7 For the lips of a priest should
guard knowledge, and people should
seek instruction from his mouth, for he
is the messenger of the LORD of hosts.
8 But you have turned aside from the
way; you have caused many to stumble
by your instruction; you have corrupted
the covenant of Levi, says the LORD of
hosts, 9 and so I make you despised and
abased before all the people, inasmuch
as you have not kept my ways but have
shown partiality in your instruction.

but the Torah prohibits them. According to Leviticus, burnt offerings, offerings of well-being, and sin and guilt offerings must be "without blemish" (Lev 1:3, 10; 3:1, 6; 4:3, 23, 28, 32; 5:15, 18; 6:6). The phrase's frequency indicates an emphasis on the required wholeness and perfection of sacrificial animals. Instead, people bring defective animals, and the priests take them. Strictly from an economic perspective, sacrificing the less useful animals makes sense, allowing the people to preserve the healthier animals for mating or other financial purposes. Priests eat sin and guilt offerings (Lev 6:29, 7:6), while the priest and the one bringing the animal share well-being offerings (Lev 7:28-36). But particularly with burnt offerings, which are not eaten (Lev 1:9, 13), sacrificing an animal that cannot be used for another purpose seems like a sound fiscal practice.

Apparently, however, God is not an economist, because he considers the inferior animals "an affront to God's parenthood."[3] Regarding the imperfect beasts, the prophet asks, "Try presenting that to your governor;

3. Paul L. Redditt, *Haggai, Zechariah, Malachi* (Grand Rapids, MI: Eerdmans, 1995), 165.

will he be pleased with you or show you favor? says the LORD of hosts" (Mal 1:8). The implied answer is no, and with it a piqued deity rejects the sacrifices as well: "I have no pleasure in you, says the Lord of hosts, and I will not accept an offering from your hands" (Mal 1:10). Any attempts to receive God's favor will be unsuccessful under these conditions, as opposed to the success of men like Jacob in earlier times.[4] Scholars note that the irregular sacrifices make up the primary problem in this oracle.[5] The bad offerings cannot be justified because of God's status according to Mal 1:11: "For from the rising of the sun to its setting my name is great among the nations, and in every place incense is offered to my name, and a pure offering, for my name is great among the nations, says the LORD of hosts." God claims that his glory merits glorious sacrifices.

Malachi 1:11 has led to much scholarly debate regarding the identity of the worshipers "among the nations" and the extent of God's greatness. Weyde writes, "Mal 1:11 has puzzled scholars."[6] Are the worshipers Jews or Gentiles, and is the worship now or in the age to come?[7] Without taking a definitive position, David L. Petersen states that a powerful God receives worship outside of Jerusalem. Weyde concludes that the worshipers consist of diaspora Jews; they properly honor God, while the Jerusalem priests do not. Åke Viberg persuasively argues that the verse is a metaphor designed to exalt God's image and contrast it with the priests' bad behavior. Reading Mal 1:11 with 1:14 ("For I am a great King, says the LORD of hosts, and my name is reverenced among the nations"), Innocent Himbaza reaches a similar conclusion—the author of Malachi uses the language of greatness and power, traditionally associated with

4. Helmut Utzschneider, "Die Schriftprophetie und die Frage nach dem Ende der Prophetie. Uberlegungen anhand von Mal 1,6 – 2,16," *ZAW* 104 (1992): 383–84.

5. David L. Petersen, *Zechariah 9–14 and Malachi: A Commentary* (Louisville, KY: Westminster John Knox, 1995), 183; Weyde, *Prophecy and Teaching*, 138.

6. Ibid., 146.

7. Redditt, *Haggai, Zechariah, Malachi*, 165–66; Åke Viberg, "Wakening a Sleeping Metaphor: A New Interpretation of Malachi 1.11," *TynBul* 45 (1994): 300–307. In the early church period, Mal 1.11 functioned as a Eucharistic prooftext; the spread of churches fulfilled the prophecy that God would receive offerings everywhere. C. John Collins, "The Eucharist as Christian Sacrifice: How Patristic Authors Can Help Us Read the Bible," *WTJ* 66 (2004): 5. The idea of Eucharist as sacrifice in connection with Mal 1 first appeared in the *Didache* and then the writings of Justin Martyr, Irenaeus, and Tertullian to support orthodox Christian ritual against Jews and heretics. In a twist, the Gnostic Gospel of Judas utilizes Mal 1 to claim that the orthodox practice of Eucharist is an error that God will punish on judgment day. Johann Konrad Schwarz, "Die Kultpolemik im 'Evangelium des Judas,'" *Early Christianity* 3 (2012): 79–84.

Persian kings throughout the empire, and appropriates it for God, the true Almighty.[8]

The argument that the claims about the extent of YHWH worship operate as metaphors fits best within the passage itself, which already contains an abundance of rhetorical flourishes. The questions God attributes to the priests in Mal 1:6-7 establish the contrast between an injured deity and misbehaving servants. The sarcastic question in Mal 1:8, which suggests that the people would not dare to give such unworthy animals to their human governor, makes God's sense of their disdain for God even more apparent. And right before the insistence on God's greatness in Mal 1:11, the prophet puts a dramatic exclamation in God's mouth: "Oh, that someone among you would shut the temple doors, so that you would not kindle fire on my altar in vain!" (Mal 1:10). If God were a character in a play, one could envision him wringing his hands while uttering that line. The insistence on God's greatness functions as a justification for the criticism of the priests, and an all-powerful God cannot receive anything less than the absolute best animals available. Simply put, God deserves respect and honor, because he says so and other people treat him accordingly; therefore, his own designated servants should give God his due.

Lest the priests find God's appeal to honor uninspiring, the second half of the oracle begins with a threat or specifically a "command" (Mal 2:1). If the priests fail to change their ways, God promises, "I will send the curse on you and I will curse your blessings" (Mal 2:2). Similar to Hag 1, Mal 2 claims that the curse has begun: "indeed I have already cursed them, because you do not lay it to heart" (2:2). And worse may come. Malachi 2:3 warns that "I will rebuke your offspring, and spread dung on your faces, the dung of your offerings, and I will put you out of my presence." In Leviticus, priests burn the dung of sacrificial animals outside of the altar space (4:11-12); in the case of sin offerings on Yom Kippur, "their dung shall be consumed in fire. The one who burns them shall wash his clothes and bathe his body in water, and afterward may come into the camp" (Lev 16:27-28). Typically, any uncleanness that requires washing and bathing for removal, including touching unclean animals or making contact with unclean houses or people, only renders

8. Petersen, *Zechariah 9–14 and Malachi*, 183–84; Weyde, *Prophecy and Teaching*, 149; Viberg, "Wakening a Sleeping Metaphor," 307–18; Innocent Himbaza, "<<*YHWH Seba'ot* deviant le grand roi>>. Une interpretation de Ml 1,6-14 à la lumière du context perse," *VT* 623 (2012): 357–68.

the person unclean "until the evening" (Lev 11:24-40; 14:43-47; 15:1-12, 16-23). Some scholars, however, characterize the divine threat in Mal 2:3 as devastating. Paul L. Redditt writes, "The picture of God rubbing offal onto the faces of the priests is shocking. The effect of such contact would be to render them ritually unclean and, hence, unable to offer the sacrifices."[9] Petersen concurs, stating that "no more radical condemnation of the Aaronid line can be imagined."[10] While having a face full of feces can minimally be described as unpleasant, the unpleasantness has a basic solution—wash your face. Ritual uncleanness disappears with ritual purification. No matter how disgusting a dung-smeared face will be or how humiliated a priest will feel, the punishment is temporary.

Perhaps the prophet recognizes that a divine threat of future temporary uncleanness lacks authority, because the tone of the text quickly shifts in Mal 2:4-7. Instead of threats as incentives for behavioral change, God appeals to past positive behavior, specifically a description of "my covenant with Levi" (Mal 2:4). This covenant has been the subject of much scholarly discourse, and the prophet outlines it at length:

> My covenant with him was a covenant of life and well-being, which I gave him; this called for reverence, and he revered me and stood in awe of my name. True instruction was in his mouth, and no wrong was found on his lips. He walked with me in integrity and uprightness, and he turned many from iniquity. For the lips of a priest should guard knowledge, and people should seek instruction from his mouth, for he is the messenger of the LORD of hosts. (Mal 2:5-7)

According to the covenant terms, God gives the priests חיים ושלום ("life and peace"); in exchange, the priests are supposed to give God the respect that cannot be found in Mal 1. The priests are also supposed to act as flawless teachers, presenting wise and proper counsel and having the ear of the community. Again, this behavior contrasts sharply with Mal 1:12, where God asserts that the priests "say that the LORD's table is polluted, and the food for it may be despised." Such a statement is the opposite of "true instruction" (Mal 2:6).

For the last twenty years, scholars have asked two questions about this covenant. To whom does it apply and what is it? Regarding the first question, Redditt suggests that the mention of Levi "is another case of the prophet's deliberate refusal to make distinctions within the post-exilic

9. Redditt, *Haggai, Zechariah, Malachi*, 168.
10. Petersen, *Zechariah 9–14 and Malachi*, 189.

priesthood."[11] Petersen connects Mal 2 with Neh 13 and argues that the covenant in Malachi distinguishes between obedient Levites and disobedient priests; Helmut Utzschneider makes a similar argument three years earlier.[12] Weyde splits the difference, concluding that Mal 2 contrasts priests and Levi but not priests and Levites, although "a distinction existed" between the two groups.[13] Reading the passage intratextually, the prophet criticizes priests as a whole for breaking their deal with God and not following the example of their ancestor Levi. Any hierarchy of Aaronid priests and non-Aaronid Levites does not appear in Mal 2.

Intertextually, however, the covenant in Mal 2 has no definitive or conclusive parallel or reference. No other place in the Hebrew Bible mentions such a covenant with Levi so directly or explicitly.[14] Jeremiah 33:21 notes that God calls it "my covenant with my ministers the Levites."[15] Nehemiah 13:29 defines "the priesthood" as "the covenant of the priests and the Levites."[16] Russell Fuller suggests that Deut 33:8-11 may be one of the traditions echoed in Mal 2, although the prophet does not cite it specifically.[17] Deuteronomy 33:10 grants Levi the Urim and Thummin and states the job of the priests: "They teach Jacob your ordinances, and Israel your law; they place incense before you, and whole burnt offerings on your altar" (Deut 33:10).[18] Ruth Scoralick notes parallels between Hos 4 and Mal 2; the people should be knowledgeable, but are not because the priests do not teach them (Hos 4:6; cf. Mal 2:7-8).[19] From Malachi's perspective, priests clearly have specific duties and obligations. Allowing

11. Redditt, *Haggai, Zechariah, Malachi*, 168.

12. Petersen, *Zechariah 9–14 and Malachi*, 192–93; Utzschneider, "Schriftprophetie," 390.

13. Weyde, *Prophecy and Teaching*, 183–84.

14. Redditt, *Haggai, Zechariah, Malachi*, 168; Petersen, *Zechariah 9–14 and Malachi*, 188; Weyde, *Prophecy and Teaching*, 176.

15. Redditt, *Haggai, Zechariah, Malachi*, 168.

16. Petersen, *Zechariah 9–14 and Malachi*, 179.

17. Russell Fuller, "The Blessing of Levi in Dtn 33, Mal 2, and Qumran," in *Konsequente Traditionsgeschichte: Festschrift für Klaus Baltzer zum 65. Geburtstag*, ed. Rüdiger Bartelmus, Thomas Krüger, and Helmut Utzschneider (Göttingen: Vandenhoeck & Ruprecht, 1993), 32, 38, 43; cf. Jon L. Berquist, *Judaism in Persia's Shadow: A Social and Historical Approach* (Minneapolis: Fortress, 1995), 98.

18. Sirach 45:17 makes a similar point about the priestly teaching office – "In his [God's] commandments he gave him [Aaron] authority and statutes and judgments, to teach Jacob the testimonies, and to enlighten Israel with his law."

19. Ruth Scoralick, "Priester als <<Boten>> Gottes (Mal 2,7)?: Zum Priester- und ProphetenBild des Zwölfprophetenbuches," in *Die unwiderstehliche Wahrheit: Studien*

the sacrifice of imperfect animals, they "have corrupted the covenant of Levi" (Mal 2:8). The bulk of the corruption may be the failure to reject the animals for the sake of privileging their own stomachs; the priests literally "feed on the sin of my people; they are greedy for their iniquity" (Hos 4:8).[20] Rather than risk hunger, the priests sacrifice whatever they receive, triggering the prophet's lengthy complaint.

Does the complaint serve its purpose of changing behavior? The issue of sacrifices returns in Mal 2:17–3:5.[21] Apparently, God is still so irritated about the improper offerings that he decides to send a representative down to irritate the priests. Beyond Malachi, the Jerusalem temple itself survives until 70 CE, and sacrifices continued as well. Written in the second century BCE, Sir 45:14-16 mentions the twice daily sacrifices that priests should offer forever. Leviticus and three of the gospels describe bird sellers in the temple, and such sellers were necessary for poor travelers who could not afford sheep or goats (Lev 1:14-17, 5:11-13; Matt 21:12; Mark 11:15; John 2:14-16). Less clear, however, is whether priestly attitudes changed, and the passage in Malachi suggests that the prophet's rhetoric may have been ineffective in that regard. In the middle of the divine complaint, the prophet puts the following line in the priests' mouths: "'What a weariness this is,' you say, and you sniff at me, says the Lord of hosts" (Mal 1:13). The priests take little interest in offering the sacrifices and even less interest in offering the correct ones. The people will echo this lack of enthusiasm in later oracles. Also, the text's claims about the now reduced status of the priestly class fall flat. Malachi 2:2 states that God has "already cursed" the priests' blessings. How? If people continue to bring animals, then the priests continue to eat. Unless the sick animals taste bad or deliver smaller portion sizes, the priests lose nothing by maintaining the sacrificial status quo, however frustrating from God's perspective. The prophet tells the priests that God says "I make you despised and abased before all the people, inasmuch as you have not kept my ways but have shown partiality in your instruction" (Mal 2:9). How is this so? Perhaps the inferior animals signify disrespect, but if the priests do not take offense, then is their treatment fully offensive?

Throughout the text, God demands honor and accuses his representatives of failing to obtain that honor for him. The priests, however, care

---

zur alttestamentlichen Prophetie: Festschrift für Arndt Meinhold, ed. Rüdiger Lux and Ernst-Joachim Waschke (Leipzig: Evangelische Verlagsanstalt, 2006), 428.

20. Ibid.

21. Petersen, *Zechariah 9–14 and Malachi*, 211; Weyde, *Prophecy and Teaching*, 301.

little about being treated badly. The text calls on them to feel shame, and they do not. The male-dominated hierarchy of God-priests-laity is now unstable, because the men below refuse to honor the man above. God's attempt at repair consists only of complaints and threats, similar to the exasperated mother who exclaims, "Just wait until your father gets home!" God is supposed to be the father, however, and whether his arrival strikes fear in the hearts of his children remains to be seen. For now, the priests see God as a weak mother and not a powerful father; they shame God without remorse or apology, and shame in the ancient world belongs in a woman's realm. To the priests, God appears to be fighting like a girl—and losing.

Malachi 2:10-16

Is God a Girl?

Malachi 2:10-16, without question, offers more interpretive challenges than any other passage addressed in this volume. The words themselves allow for multiple translations and therefore multiple interpretations. Nevertheless, whether read literally as a critique of intermarriage and/or divorce, or figuratively as a prophetic complaint against syncretism and/or apostasy, or as both, the text freely lends itself to feminist analyses. Although I am partial to a figurative reading for Mal 2:10-12 and a literal reading against divorce for Mal 2:13-16, any interpretation of the passage is rich in possible meanings. There may be a marriage metaphor with God as the mistreated wife, a defense of monogamy and aggrieved first wives by the masculine witness YHWH, and/or a defense of endogamy. Textual ambiguity results in textual support for these possibilities, so all of them will be discussed here for their contributions to a conversation about gender and power in Malachi.

Malachi 2:10-16 contains several obscure phrases with varying degrees of difficulty; all of them will influence the following discussion. First, is "the daughter of a foreign god" (Mal 2:11) an allusion to an ancient Near Eastern goddess or a description of a non-Israelite woman? Second, ער, translated by NRSV as "any to witness" in Mal 2:12, is a correction of the Hebrew word ער, "arouse," to the word עד, "witness," by the NRSV translators. The correction occurs by changing the second consonant in the word from a ר (r) to a ד (d). Third, Mal 2:15 begins with an ambiguous

Mal 2:10-16

10 Have we not all one father? Has not one God created us? Why then are we faithless to one another, profaning the covenant of our ancestors? 11 Judah has been faithless, and abomination has been committed in Israel and in Jerusalem; for Judah has profaned the sanctuary of the LORD, which he loves, and has married the daughter of a foreign god. 12 May the LORD cut off from the tents of Jacob anyone who does this—any to witness or answer, or to bring an offering to the LORD of hosts.

13 And this you do as well: You cover the LORD's altar with tears, with weeping and groaning because he no longer regards the offering or accepts it with favor at your hand. 14 You ask, "Why does he not?" Because the LORD was a witness between you and the wife of your youth, to whom you have been faithless, though she is your companion and your wife by covenant. 15 Did not one God make her? Both flesh and spirit are his. And what does the one God desire? Godly offspring. So look to yourselves, and do not let anyone be faithless to the wife of his youth. 16 For I hate divorce, says the LORD, the God of Israel, and covering one's garment with violence, says the LORD of hosts. So take heed to yourselves and do not be faithless.

question and answer. The Hebrew phrase ולא אחד עשה translated as "Did not one God make her?" can also be translated as "Has he not made one?" or simply as "He made," if the words "not" and "one" are additions to the text, as BHS suggests. No clear words for "God" or "her" appear, however, in the Hebrew. "Both flesh and spirit are his" is a correction by the translators of the original Hebrew, ושאר רוח לו, "and a remnant of spirit was his." The correction comes from changing the vowels in the Hebrew word "remnant" to the vowels for the word "flesh." Fourth, "I hate divorce" in Mal 2:16 is another translator correction; while the Hebrew text has שנא, "he hates," BHS suggests that the verb should read שנאתי, "I hate." How one translates these phrases determines whether the passage may refer to intermarriage or apostasy and whether the prophet claims that God opposes divorce because of the unity of a married couple or whether the man who divorces harms himself but does not arouse God's hate by his actions.

The verbs used as warnings against abandoning a first wife complicate the text further. The prophet asks the men to "look to yourselves" (ונשמרתם) and "take heed to yourselves" (ונשמרתם) (Mal 2:15-16). The same verb is used here, in a passive imperative form, which usually means "to be on one's guard." But the problem is that the verb then appears with the phrase "about your breath/spirit" (ברוחכם). In Mal 2:15, the phrase is considered an addition, according to BHS, and the entire unit in Mal

2:16—"be on your guard about your breath/spirit"—is thought to be an addition from the previous verse. The addition matters because, if read together, both verses suggest that divorce is a serious event that could endanger a husband's life. But it is noteworthy that the NRSV does not translate the phrase "about your breath/spirit," saying only that the men should examine themselves, minimizing the text in a way that the JPS translation ("so be careful of your life-breath"), for example, does not.

Two common literal readings of Mal 2:10-16 appear in scholarly discourse: that the text condemns intermarriage and that the text condemns divorce. For example, Adam S. van der Woude argues that the passage echoes Ezra 9–10 and Neh 13 in their opposition to intermarriage between Jewish men and non-Jewish women, or the " 'daughters of a foreign god,' i.e., foreign women who do not worship the Lord."[1] Regarding divorce, van der Woude asserts, in contrast to the common reading of Mal 2:16 as a critique of divorce (literally "to send away" in Hebrew), that "it must sincerely be doubted whether in Old Testament times even a prophet would have denounced divorce as a crime. Deuteronomy 24 tells against this interpretation."[2] Specifically, Deut 24:1-4 allows a man to divorce his wife, but if she remarries and then her second husband divorces her, the first husband "is not permitted to take her again" (Deut 24:4). The Torah passage may not be a helpful lens through which to view Malachi, however, because the prophetic passage does not call divorce a crime; instead, it characterizes the dissolution of a first marriage as "faithless" (Mal 2:14-16). This may not be the same as unlawful.

Karl M. Weyde also argues that the Malachi passage opposes intermarriage. He claims that union "with a woman who worships a foreign god is an abomination, because it *leads to* idolatry."[3] Malachi 2:16 rejects divorce only within the context of intermarriage. Jewish men should not divorce their Jewish wives in order to marry non-Jewish women, because, based on Gen 2, God created male and female in order to maintain a holy community separated from idol worshipers. If this is the case, then what could have been a pro-woman argument against divorce is mitigated

1. Adam S. van der Woude, "Malachi's Struggle for a Pure Community: Reflections on Malachi 2:10-16," in *Tradition and Re-Interpretation in Jewish and Early Christian Literature: Essays in Honour of Jürgen C.M. Lebram*, ed. J.W. Van Henten, H. J. De Jonge, P.T. Van Rooden, and J.W. Wesselius (Leiden: Brill, 1986), 67.

2. Ibid., 71.

3. Karl William Weyde, *Prophecy and Teaching: Prophetic Authority, Form Problems, and the Use of Traditions in the Book of Malachi* (Berlin: Walter de Gruyter, 2000), 232–33.

and then muted by concerns about ethnic purity. Other than Israelite wives, the prophet shows no interest in the plight of wives who may be divorced and abandoned at their husbands' discretion. The non-Israelite wives, as Ezra suggests, could be sent away with their children to fend for themselves (Ezra 10:3-5, 11, 44).

Markus Zehnder makes the same claims as Weyde, but with two twists: that God is the bride and that it is the rejected wives who cry at the altar. First, Weyde asserts that the text should be read literally because "a figurative interpretation would result in YHWH taking the role of a bride which contradicts the *normal* reverse order in which Israel is the bride and YHWH the groom (cf. Hos., Jer., Ezek., DtJes)."[4] "Normal" suggests that God can only be portrayed as a bridegroom or as a man in general, but in prophetic literature this is not the case. Second Isaiah compares God's restoration of the exiles to a woman's labor pains (42:14-16) and God's love for Israel as stronger than the mother-child bond (49:15-16). Therefore, precedent exists for using gendered imagery for God that need not be masculine imagery. Also, in the marriage metaphor, God as authoritative husband often towers over his disobedient and adulterous wife Israel. God threatens her with stripping and starvation (Hos 2:2-3), divorce (Jer 3:1-9), and death at her lovers' hands (Ezek 16:35-43; 23:22-27). Chastened and rebuked, she either calls to her husband for a renewal of the marriage, which she receives (Hos 2:7, 14-20), or is silenced into submission (Ezek 16:61-63). Even in the less graphic imagery of Second Isaiah, God initiates a separation from his wife due to their misbehaving children (50:1), and this separation, now over, was motivated by God the husband's intense anger (54:4-8). In contrast, God demands proper respect in Mal 1, yet respect is not forthcoming. The priests question the critique of their offerings and, unlike the bride in Ezekiel, they talk back: " 'What a weariness this is,' you say, and you sniff at me, says the LORD of hosts" (Mal 1:13). In this context, returning to the earlier marriage metaphor goes against Malachi's characterization of God as annoyed but also apparently less able to compel obedience.

Zehnder's reading of Mal 2:13 offers the second twist: the abandoned wives, not the men whose offerings God rejects, "cover the LORD's altar

4. Markus Zehnder, "A Fresh Look at Malachi II 13–16," *VT* 53 (2003): 228; emphasis mine. Paul L. Redditt concurs, arguing that nowhere else in the Hebrew Bible alludes to God as a wife. Unlike Zehnder, however, Redditt thinks that the passage refers to divorce in general and not strictly divorce for the purposes of intermarriage. Paul L. Redditt, *Haggai, Zechariah, Malachi* (Grand Rapids, MI: Eerdmans, 1995), 171–73, 75.

with tears." In spite of the second masculine plural verb תעשו ("you [men] cover"), Zehnder portrays the wives as weeping and wailing at the altar, figuratively at least; "the covering of the altar by the women's tears is a figurative expression for the mourning with which the deceived wives seek the presence of YHWH."[5] Although Zehnder opposes a metaphorical reading of the passage, he makes an exception here. This interpretation reinforces two gender stereotypes: God as alpha male and Israel as a wife or damsel in distress.

Those who read Mal 2:10-16 figuratively argue for a new marriage metaphor, with unfaithful Judah as the husband and God as the abandoned wife. Julia M. O'Brien states that Malachi emphasizes the father/son relationship between God and the people, which is "one of sheer power."[6] But this relationship breaks down in Mal 2:11, which personifies Judah first as female and then as male, based on the gender of the Hebrew verbs. With the shift, Judah becomes the husband; by implication, God becomes feminine, overturning the marriage metaphor and God's status as masculine head of household in Mal 1.[7] David L. Petersen interprets the passage as a protest against Israelite worship of Asherah, "the daughter of a foreign god" in Mal 2:11. Regarding Mal 2:14, Petersen argues as follows: "The 'wife of your youth' is, I suggest, Yahweh, the deity whom Israel is supposed to venerate; and this in contradistinction to the improper deity, the goddess Asherah, another possible female spouse already identified in Mal 2:11. Yahweh is here viewed as the spouse of Israel, but this time a female spouse of the male Israel. The gender of the spouses is different from the book of Hosea, in which Yahweh was the male spouse and Israel the female."[8] The text therefore argues against any dissolution of the marriage between Judah and God.[9]

Danna Nolan Fewell states, "Feminist theory insists that singular definitions are misleading and limiting."[10] With that in mind, a feminist

5. Zehnder, "A Fresh Look," 234.

6. Julia M. O'Brien, "Judah as Wife and Husband: Deconstructing Gender in Malachi," *JBL* 115 (1996): 242.

7. Ibid., 247–49.

8. David L. Petersen, *Zechariah 9–14 and Malachi* (Louisville, KY: Westminster John Knox, 1995), 203.

9. Ibid., 205.

10. Danna Nolan Fewell, "Reading the Bible Ideologically: Feminist Criticism," in *To Each Its Own Meaning: Biblical Criticisms and Their Applications*, rev. and expanded, ed. Steven L. McKenzie and Stephen R. Haynes (Louisville, KY: Westminster John Knox, 1999), 268.

interpretation of this passage may take the literal and figurative arguments into account without assuming that one argument excludes the other. Three scholars offer this both/and approach to the text. Beth Glazier-McDonald argues that "the daughter of a foreign god" in Mal 2:11 refers literally to a non-Israelite woman and metaphorically to a goddess. Therefore, Malachi complains about intermarriage and apostasy, with the aggrieved first wife as both a Jewish woman and God.[11] Utilizing the Hebrew "arouse" in Mal 2:12 instead of the NRSV correction "to witness," Glazier-McDonald also concludes that the text, like other prophetic texts (Hos 2:5, 3:3; Jer 3:6-8), calls Judah a whore. This time, however, the whore is a man and not a woman.[12] Herbert Donner divides the passage into poetry (vv. 10, 11a, 13aα, 14, 16a) and prose (11b, 12, 13aβ, 15, 16b).[13] Because of the figurative language in Mal 2:11b and the linguistic difficulties of Mal 2:15, the categorization of these verses as prose is debatable. Donner, however, uses the distinction between poetry and prose in Mal 2 to develop a thought-provoking thesis: The poetry opposes divorce as a solution to intermarriage, against Ezra, but the prose condemns mixed marriages as sacrilegious, in support of Ezra's and Nehemiah's position. The prose later became the text through which the poetry was read and understood.

Martin A. Shields's argument may be the most persuasive. He argues that Mal 2:10-12 figuratively protests syncretism and Mal 2:13-16 literally opposes divorce.[14] The entire passage, he adds, has one "principal concern . . . faithlessness."[15] Not only is the word included in the NRSV heading for this section, but the Hebrew verb בגד, which is accurately translated as "to be faithless," appears in five of the seven verses in the passage "but nowhere else in Malachi."[16] The text complains about two kinds of faithless behavior: Judah's worship of a goddess, based on a figurative interpreta-

11. Beth Glazier-McDonald, "Intermarriage, Divorce, and the *Bāt-'ēl nēkār*: Insights into Mal 2:10-16," *JBL* 106 (1987): 603–11.

12. Beth Glazier-McDonald, "Malachi 2:12: *'ēr wĕ'ōneh* – another look," *JBL* 105 (1986): 297–98.

13. Herbert Donner, "Ein Vorschlag zum Verständnis von Maleachi 2, 10-16," in *Von Gott reden: Beiträge zur Theologie und Exegese des Alten Testaments. Festschrift für Siegfried Wanger zum 65. Geburtstag*, ed. Dieter Vieweger und Ernst-JoachimWaschke (Neukirchen-Vluyn: Neukirchener, 1995), 97–103.

14. Martin A. Shields, "Syncretism and Divorce in Malachi 2, 10-16," *ZAW* 111 (1999): 68–69.

15. Ibid., 69.

16. Ibid.

tion of "the daughter of a foreign god" in Mal 2:11; and divorce, based on a literal interpretation of Mal 2:13-16.[17] Shields, however, does not bring Ezra and Nehemiah's condemnation of mixed marriages into Malachi.

Although all of these readings have merit, Shields's division of the text works best for two reasons. First, Mal 2:11 describes a state of religious uncleanness. "Judah has profaned the sanctuary of the Lord" by rejecting YHWH as his bride and taking a goddess instead. Jeremiah 2 describes the marriage as one between groom YHWH and bride Israel, but the source of the marital discord is the same as in Malachi. The people worship other gods instead of YHWH (Jer 2:4-37). Consequently, the people in Malachi will have their sacrifices rejected because of their idolatry; similarly, the people in Jeremiah, who God says have "defiled my land and made my heritage an abomination" (2:7), will suffer death and destruction, and their prayers will go unanswered (2:27-30, 35-37). Also, Ezek 7–10 argues that idolatry has contaminated God's house to the point where God abandons it and the people. And it is idolatry, described as adultery in Ezek 16 and 23, which triggers the husband God's violent punishment of the wife Israel. Malachi's imagery portrays God as a wife, and the punishment is much less severe; just as an offended wife might not immediately accept her apologetic husband's attempt at a peace offering, the injured YHWH spurns the people's offerings. The complaint, however, remains the same: the contaminating influence of apostasy.

Second, Mal 2:13 suggests a division of the text with its opening phrase, "And this you do as well." BHS argues that this phrase, along with Mal 2:11b-12, is probably an addition. If this is the case, then the text has no marriage metaphor with God as bride, and the passage complains only about the faithlessness of men divorcing women. BHS, however, offers no explanation for its proposal, and the LXX includes the proposed additions, along with 4QXII^a from Qumran. 4QXII^a even includes the correction of Mal 2:12 that appears in the NRSV translation: "any to witness."[18] Therefore, the existing Hebrew text implies that Mal 2:11-12 outlines one problem, and the rest of the passage explains another problem. Even if "as well" is the only addition, which BHS also raises as a possibility, the phrase still reads "And this you do." The language suggests some type of transition, which allows for a different explanation of the second half of the passage.

17. Ibid., 72–73, 78.

18. Russell Fuller, "Text-Critical Problems in Malachi 2:10-16," *JBL* 110 (1991): 47, 50–51.

If God cuts off the idolatrous men who dare "to bring an offering to the LORD of hosts" (Mal 2:12), God also rejects the offerings of any man who is faithless to his wife (Mal 2:13-14). The text speaks of "the wife of your youth . . . your companion and your wife by covenant" (Mal 2:14), with no mention of ethnicity. So, reading Ezra and Nehemiah into Malachi's context, while possible, is not necessary. The passage may critique divorce without critiquing intermarriage.

Finally, I have devoted much space to what the text says, but what the text does not say is also interesting. Prophetic condemnation often includes dire consequences for the disobedient. The apostasy in Hosea, Jeremiah, and Ezekiel, for example, brings exile, as God avenges God's violated honor. Here, however, no vengeance takes place. The prophet hopes that God punishes the idolaters: "may the LORD cut off from the tents of Jacob anyone who does this" (Mal 2:12). Also, God says that those who mistreat their wives should "look to yourselves" and "take heed to yourselves" (Mal 2:15-16). These are not strong words. BDB suggests the verb used here, שמר, "to be on one's guard," in this context may also imply "on peril of your life."[19] Without the possible implication, however, the warning sounds more like an empty threat. God does not like divorce and tells men to examine their conduct. So what? The people in Malachi have been talking back to God's spokesperson from the beginning, and they continue to do so here: "Why does he not [accept our offerings]?" (Mal 2:14). Two of the next three passages in Malachi include the people's questions of divine retribution, or whether God rewards the righteous and punishes the wicked. If the people challenge this principle, then they may also challenge the prophet's claim that God opposes their behavior. Even if God dislikes their actions, what can God really do about it and who will stop the people from doing what they please?

The previously unshakable image of God as the patriarch who commands respect and must be obeyed now totters on its pedestal. O'Brien, concluding her argument about God as Judah's mistreated bride in Mal 2:11, writes, "Devastatingly for Malachi's argument, if God is feminine, then God is not father at all."[20] Although personified as a man in the second part of the passage, God's masculinity is under attack. God seems less powerful and less forceful here, perhaps even stereotypically effeminate.

19. BDB 1037.

20. O'Brien, "Judah as Wife and Husband," 249.

Malachi and the Complicated Marriage(s) Malachi 2:10-16

Malachi 2:10-16 is perhaps the most interesting (or confusing) passage in the Hebrew Bible that deals with marriage as a metaphor. In this passage there are three specific references to marriage: one that is characterized badly, one that is characterized well, and one that admonishes divorce. Together, these three marriage references create an interesting and difficult picture to consider, especially given that in both the bad marriage and the good marriage Israel is characterized as the husband.

Like many prophetic writings of rebuke, this passage in Malachi seems to follow a simple formula: enumerate the wrongs committed and explain the road to repentance. The first, and seemingly foremost, wrong committed by Israel in this passage is a marriage in verse 11. In other prophetic passages Israel (or Judah) is accused of marrying other gods—a metaphor for disloyalty to the God of Israel by way of religious practices that honor gods that were worshiped outside of the Israelite community in the Ancient Near East.

This passage, however, does not specify that Israel has married other gods but rather the daughters of other gods. While this could easily still be metaphor, it could also be literal—Malachi might be condemning the men of Judah for marrying women who did not belong to the cult of the God of Israel. In practice this is much the same issue: whether or not Israel (or the men therein) have metaphorically married other gods or literally married women who worship other gods, there is an understanding of deviant religious practice. Generally speaking, where ancient religions were concerned, home worship was a key piece of the religious life, which would make a marriage between two people of different religions a difficult thing as the home would then be saturated by religious objects and practices from different religious cultures.

Marriage makes its second appearance in verse 14, and it is this marriage metaphor that is, perhaps, the most inscrutable marriage metaphor that appears in the prophetic writings. Several possible theories exist concerning who was this wife of Israel's youth, and each comes with its strengths and weaknesses as a theory. For example, the wife of Israel's youth was possibly a real person. Perhaps the issue at hand is that Israel has married women from Israel and God is angry because Israel then married women who were not part of the same religious cult. For religious reasons this situation might make sense, since, as was discussed above, a mixed religious household in the ancient world was problematic. It does not seem likely, however, that enough men in Israel and Judah would have taken wives in their own community and then subsequently married women outside the religious community for God to feel the need to condemn the people as a whole for the practice.

The alternative—namely, that the wife of Israel's youth is actually God—is also not a perfect fit. To begin with, it seems odd that God might have borne witness to a marriage that God was also involved in. Indeed, the mental gymnastics required to make a scenario in which God was both witness and participant seems too much of a stretch for a message that should, at least theoretically, have been quite clear to Malachi's audience in the ancient world. If, however, the argument is made (and accepted) that God, as the ultimate witness, could indeed both witness and participate in an event like a covenantal marriage, that would mean the passage is suggesting that God is Israel's wife.

This metaphor would be a unique one in the Hebrew Bible and one that has myriad interesting implications. While God and Israel certainly appear as a married couple in several prophetic instances, God is always the husband in this metaphor, while Israel is the wife. In the pervasive patriarchy of the ancient world, this husband-wife metaphor is the only one that makes ideological sense: the husband (God) has the power in the relationship while the wife (Israel) is subject to the power of her husband. The metaphor is a very tidy one for the prophets to use, as it does seem to very closely mirror the metaphorical relationship between God and God's people in the world of the Hebrew Bible. Israel has a will of its own and is capable of disloyalty and disobedience toward its husband, God, and God is very unappreciative when disloyalty and unfaithfulness occur.

The flipped metaphor, which very well may be what is happening in Malachi, is much less tidy. If the wife of Israel's youth is indeed God, then, in Malachi, Israel actually has the culturally imbued power in the relationship. While God as the wife and God's people as the husband is perhaps not such a crazy metaphor in the modern world, where power is, at least theoretically, more equal between partners, in the ancient world the suggestion that God's people might have more power in the relationship than God is quite shocking.

The whole scenario becomes even more interesting in the next verses. Verse 15 urges the people of Israel not to forsake the wife of their youth, whoever or whatever that may be, but verse 16 goes even further, claiming that God detests divorce and that, apparently, no marriage should be ended, for the idea of divorce in itself is extremely displeasing to God. While this might make sense in light of the marriage spoken about in verse 14, it seems especially confusing when verse 11 is factored into the equation. For if God hates divorce, does that mean Israel is meant to stay married to the foreign gods (or the women who worship them), as well? This scenario certainly seems to be the case, which is very difficult to wrap the mind around.

Rebecca M. Jones

Malachi 2:17–3:5

Divine Masculinity Restored

Malachi 2:17–3:5 picks up where Mal 1:6–2:9 leaves off, continuing and expanding the previous oracle's threat. Because the priests will not behave, a divinely sponsored messenger will come to put them in order and restore proper sacrifices. After the priests' punishment, God will come in person to judge all other sinners. Scholars have focused on two interrelated issues in this passage: the possible redaction history of Mal 3:1-4 and the identities of the messenger, the Lord, and the messenger of the covenant in Mal 3:1. Two verses, however, receive little attention: Mal 3:2, the description of the covenant messenger, and Mal 3:5, the list of those whom God will judge. From a feminist perspective, both verses say a great deal about Malachi's view of God as a paterfamilias, and a prickly one at that.

Every oracle so far has contained a specific problem (the people's questioning of God's love, inappropriate animal sacrifices, improper marriage partners), and this oracle follows the same pattern. Specifically, Malachi reports that God is worn out by questions about his righteousness. God has heard the people claim that "all who do evil are good in the sight of the Lord, and he delights in them." He has also heard them ask, "Where is the God of justice?" (Mal 2:17). These quotations turn the idea of divine retribution—God rewards the upright and punishes the sinners—completely on its head and "challenge the notions of justice that undergird much in standard Israelite wisdom, priestly, and

Mal 2:17–3:5

[17]You have wearied the LORD with your words. Yet you say, "How have we wearied him?" By saying, "All who do evil are good in the sight of the LORD, and he delights in them." Or by asking, "Where is the God of justice?"

[3:1]See, I am sending my messenger to prepare the way before me, and the LORD whom you seek will suddenly come to his temple. The messenger of the covenant in whom you delight—indeed, he is coming, says the LORD of hosts. [2]But who can endure the day of his coming, and who can stand when he appears?

For he is like a refiner's fire and like fullers' soap; [3]he will sit as a refiner and purifier of silver, and he will purify the descendants of Levi and refine them like gold and silver, until they present offerings to the LORD in righteousness. [4]Then the offering of Judah and Jerusalem will be pleasing to the LORD as in the days of old and as in former years.

[5]Then I will draw near to you for judgment; I will be swift to bear witness against the sorcerers, against the adulterers, against those who swear falsely, against those who oppress the hired workers in their wages, the widow and the orphan, against those who thrust aside the alien, and do not fear me, says the LORD of hosts.

prophetic rhetoric,"[1] similar to Job's complaints and the psalmist's concerns in Ps 73. Both texts suggest that the wicked seem to prosper, making righteous deeds moot (Job 9:24, 12:6, 21:7-15; Ps 73:2-14). Peter Suk-Hyun Kim interprets Mal 2:17 for modern readers as a call to act for justice on behalf of Korean "comfort women" and resist complacency.[2] In its postexilic context, however, the people's argument about God's neglect of righteousness and justice may explain their lack of enthusiasm regarding sacrifices. If God does not care about good deeds, then why do such deeds?[3]

According to the prophet, however, God does care. His response to the community's challenge is as follows: "See, I am sending my messenger to prepare the way before me, and the LORD whom you seek will suddenly come to his temple. The messenger of the covenant in whom

1. David L. Petersen, *Zechariah 9–14 and Malachi* (Louisville, KY: Westminster John Knox, 1995), 207.

2. Peter Suk-Hyun Kim, "Reflections on Malachi 2:17 (1994)," in *Many Voices: Multicultural Responses to the Minor Prophets*, ed. Alice Ogden Bellis (Lanham, MD: University Press of America, 1995), 82.

3. Beth Glazier-McDonald, "Mal'ak Habbêrît: The Messenger of the Covenant in Mal 3:1," *HAR* 11 (1987): 94.

you delight—indeed, he is coming, says the LORD of hosts" (Mal 3:1). And when he comes, he will bring divine justice with him, correcting errant priests and making room for God to pass sentence on all other sinners (Mal 3:3-5). While Karl W. Weyde thinks the oracle ends at Mal 3:6, which maintains God's unchanging justice and also acts as a transition to the next oracle, scholarly consensus names Mal 3:5 as the oracle's concluding verse.[4]

Most scholars argue that some redaction has taken place within Mal 2:17–3:5. Paul L. Redditt states that Mal 3:1b-4 is a redaction, with the first oracle being Mal 2:17–3:1a, 5.[5] David L. Petersen calls Mal 3:1b-4 "an interpretation" of Mal 2:17–3:1a, 5, the "original oracle."[6] Weyde agrees, noting the prevalence of first-person speech in Mal 3:1a, 5 and third-person speech in Mal 3:1b-3.[7] Additionally, as we will see, Mal 3:1b-4 uses rare and in some cases unique language, distinctive not only to the rest of the book but also to the entire Hebrew Bible, strengthening the argument in favor of redaction. Beth Glazier-McDonald, however, argues that claims for redaction are "unwarranted both linguistically and thematically."[8] Biblical passages may change addressees midstream, and Glazier-McDonald links the oracle to Mal 2:10-16, another example of the violated covenant.[9] But the examples Glazier-McDonald refers to (Isa 42:20, 54:14, 61:7; Deut 32:15; Job 16:7; Lam 3:1) are not conclusive, and the oracle can be linked to previous ones. Because Glazier-McDonald's claims about the unity of Mal 2:17–3:5 depend on her analysis of Mal 3:1, it is necessary to determine the main characters in that verse.

The only certainty within Mal 3:1 is the listing of three titles—"my messenger" (מלאכי), "the Lord" (האדון), and "the messenger of the covenant" (מלאך הברית). After that, uncertainty reigns. Are these separate char-

4. Karl William Weyde, *Prophecy and Teaching: Prophetic Authority, Form Problems, and the Use of Traditions in the Book of Malachi* (Berlin: de Gruyter, 2000), 280, 318, 321; Paul L. Redditt, *Haggai, Zechariah, Malachi* (Grand Rapids. MI: Eerdmans, 1995), 175; David L. Petersen, *Zechariah 9–14 and Malachi*, 206; Glazier-McDonald, "Mal'ak Habbêrît," 93; W. Sibley Towner, "Malachi," in *The Harper Collins Study Bible, Fully Revised and Updated*, ed. Harold W. Attridge (San Francisco: HarperSanFrancisco, 2006), 1286.

5. Redditt, *Haggai, Zechariah, Malachi*, 176–77.

6. Petersen, *Zechariah 9–14 and Malachi*, 207.

7. Weyde, *Prophecy and Teaching*, 284.

8. Glazier-McDonald, "Mal'ak Habbêrît," 95.

9. Ibid., 95–96.

acters or the same figure?[10] Redditt thinks that the identities of the Lord and the messenger are unclear in Mal 3:1, but he concludes that "it is difficult to see the Lord as anyone but God."[11] He does not distinguish between the messenger and the messenger of the covenant. Neither does Petersen, who combines the two messengers into one. He writes, "The figure is surely a prophetic one, since it was common in the postexilic period to think about prophets and messengers"; and the Lord must be God.[12] Weyde also suggests that the two messengers are one and the same, most likely a priestly figure, and "that האדון referred to YHWH, was obvious."[13] The Hebrew Bible calls God "the Lord," or האדון, and the place marker of the temple strengthens the reference in Malachi.[14] Glazier-McDonald disagrees with all of these scholars by separating the messenger from the messenger of the covenant. She then equates the Lord and the messenger of the covenant with YHWH.[15]

As debatable as Mal 3:1 is and will continue to be, the two messengers most likely represent one earthly figure, and the Lord most likely refers to God. The verse says that the messengers act as preparatory beings—the messenger "[prepares] the way before me [God]," and "the messenger of the covenant . . . is coming" (Mal 3:1). Once he has done his work, God "will suddenly come to his temple" and "draw near to you for judgment" (Mal 3:1, 5). The idea of God as possessor of the temple

10. New Testament scholars have also weighed in on the question because of the appearance of Mal 3:1 in Matt 11:10, Mark 1:2, and Luke 7:27. The Synoptic Gospels apply the Malachi text to John the Baptist, and contemporary writers have also argued that the verse is used christologically as well. James B. DeYoung ("The Function of Malachi 3.1 in Matthew 11.10: Kingdom Reality as the Hermeneutic of Jesus," in *The Gospels and the Scriptures of Israel*, ed. Craig A. Evans and W. Richard Stegner [Sheffield: Sheffield Academic Press, 1994], 69, 72, 89) states that the Lord and the covenant messenger are the same figure, Jesus. Paul B. Lee ("The Arrival Motif of Malachi's Eschatological Figures in the Gospel of Luke," *Journal of Early Christian History* 1 [2011]: 192, 199) makes the same point; the Messiah is also the Lord and covenant messenger. More broadly, Mark Goodacre ("The Evangelists' Use of the Old Testament and the Synoptic Problem," in *New Studies in the Synoptic Problem, Oxford Conference, April 2008: Essays in Honour of Christopher M. Tuckett*, ed. P. Foster, A. Gregory, J.S. Kloppenborg, and J. Verheyden [Leuven: Peeters, 2011], 284–89) uses the gospels' citation of Malachi to argue against the existence of Q.

11. Redditt, *Haggai, Zechariah, Malachi*, 176.

12. Petersen, *Zechariah 9–14 and Malachi*, 210.

13. Weyde, *Prophecy and Teaching*, 290.

14. Ibid.

15. Glazier-McDonald, "Mal'ak Habbêrît," 96–98.

and judge of the earth appears throughout the Hebrew Bible (Gen 18:25; Exod 12:12; Pss 5:7; 29:9; 42:4; 122:1; 132:8; 134:1; Joel 3:2-8; Amos 1–2). No reason exists to equate God with the messenger. Glazier-McDonald argues that "if the *'ādôn* is identified with the *mal'ak habbêrît*, the covenant enforcer, the verse assumes an unprecedented power."[16] God, however, need not be the messenger of the covenant to be incredibly and terribly powerful. God's endorsement of the messenger's actions will serve as sufficient proof of divine might.

TRANSLATION MATTERS

The description of the messenger is unique: ברית מכבסים, "he is . . . like fullers' soap" (Mal 3:2). מכבסים, the participle form of כבס, is a hapax. The verb means "to wash"; however, the NRSV translation of it as "fuller's" lends itself to multiple interpretations. A fuller may be a cloth maker or an iron worker. In keeping with the refiner imagery, Petersen suggests that ברית מכבסים could be translated as "smelter's alkali."[17] ברית appears only twice in the Hebrew Bible, Mal 3:2 and Jer 2:22. The word means lye, soap, alkali, or potash.[18] Lye and potash are used to make soap, and Jer 2:22 describes Israel as an adulterous woman whom no amount of soap [ברית] will cleanse. Alkali, however, helps to make salt and can kill most crops. At minimum, ברית מכבסים describes an industrial strength compound, fit for a messenger who will behave in almost superhuman and incredibly destructive ways.

The messenger's arrival will be unbearable,[19] bringing with it incredible amounts of heat. Petersen argues that "the fire is not one of destruction but one of purification (cf. Ezek 22:19-21; Zeph 1:18)."[20] The cited texts, however, do not support the argument. Ezekiel calls the fire that melts metal and by extension the disobedient "the fire of my [God's] wrath" (22:21). The prophet continues, "As silver is melted in a smelter, so you shall be melted in it; and you shall know that I the Lord have poured out my wrath upon you" (Ezek 22:22). Zephaniah offers no consolation, either: "Neither their silver nor their gold will be able to save them on the day of the Lord's wrath; in the fire of his passion the whole earth shall be consumed; for a full, a terrible end he will make of all the

16. Ibid., 97.
17. Petersen, *Zechariah 9–14 and Malachi*, 207.
18. BDB 141.
19. Weyde, *Prophecy and Teaching*, 295.
20. Petersen, *Zechariah 9–14 and Malachi*, 211.

inhabitants of the earth" (1:18). Redditt and Weyde conclude that describing the messenger as refiner's fire creates a punitive image,[21] and their point is well-taken. Even though Mal 3:3 calls the burning process purification for heavenly purposes, the process will hurt like hell.

The messenger "will sit as a refiner and purifier of silver, and he will purify the descendants of Levi and refine them like gold and silver" (Mal 3:3), and silver purification requires significant heat. Silver melts at 1,764°F (962°C); in order to refine silver from copper concentrate, one heats the silver, adds zinc, and then heats the silver residue to 1,450°F (800°C).[22] To place these temperatures in perspective, a person can get a third-degree burn after five seconds of contact with heat at 140°F.[23] The average temperature of a house fire is 1,100°F.[24] The messenger's job as silver refiner comes with major risks and dangers. But if God has sent him to burn up the priests, then God's anger against them has broken out like a fire. Malachi creates a destructive image; metals can survive the purification process, but humans typically cannot. What purpose does such an image serve?

The priests will be burned "until they present offerings to the Lord in righteousness. Then the offering of Judah and Jerusalem will be pleasing to the Lord as in the days of old and as in former years" (Mal 3:3-4). God still wants the proper sacrifices that the priests deny him in Mal 1. The earlier threat of temporary uncleanness and shaming gives way to torture by fire. Rhetorically, figurative language dominates the entire passage; a fiery messenger refines the priests, who are like a precious metal. But the unfriendliness and violence of the language should not be glossed over. A masculine deity punishes his unfaithful wife Israel with physical and sexual abuse in the prophetic marriage metaphor (Hos 2:2-13; Jer 2:20–4.4; Ezek 16:1-52, 23:1-49). Feminist scholars have long noted this imagery, including in *Prophets and Daniel: A Feminist Companion to the Prophets*; three essays in that volume wrestle solely with the Ezekiel

21. Redditt, *Haggai, Zechariah, Malachi*, 177; Weyde, *Prophecy and Teaching*, 297.

22. James Edward Hoffman, s. v. "silver processing", *Encyclopædia Britannica Online*, Updated 27 January 2015, http://www.britannica.com/EBchecked/topic/544891/silver-processing.

23. Burn Foundation, "Safety Facts on Scald Burns," *Burn Foundation: Prevention, Education, Treatment, Recovery*, updated 2015, http://burnfoundation.org/assets/asset_1063.pdf.

24. ABCO, "10 Things That Won't Burn in a House Fire" *ABCO Fire*, 13 October 2010, http://www.abcofire.com/2010/10/10-things-that-wont-burn-in-a-house-fire/.

texts.[25] With the notable exception of Julia M. O'Brien's work, much less attention has been paid to the violence in Malachi. Here, a masculine God sends a representative to punish his disobedient male children, the equivalent of a parent farming out a child's spanking to a third party. Ezekiel 16:37-42 and 23:10, 22-29 describe the same type of indirect divine punishment, with God as the instigator but not the perpetrator of the violence. Once God gets his way, he promises, "I will satisfy my fury on you, and my jealousy shall turn away from you; I will be calm, and will be angry no longer . . . and you shall know that I am the Lord God" (Ezek 16:42, 23:49). In Malachi, God wants his sacrificial animals "without blemish" and will use torture to get them, but he is not yet content.

After God's messenger burns the priests into submission, God turns his attention to the disobedient population as a whole. Malachi 3:5 lists two groups of sinners: those who violate others and those who violate God. While justice against the former group makes God look like a social services advocate, his own honor acts as the primary motivation. The people have questioned God's identity as "the God of justice" (Mal 2:17), and now he will reveal himself as both witness and judge (Mal 3:5).

Individuals who harm vulnerable populations, such as workers, widows, orphans, and resident aliens, will face God's indictment. The Hebrew Bible gives each group specific rights. Leviticus 19:13 prohibits an employer from holding "the wages of a laborer until morning"; without regular pay, the worker effectively becomes a slave, and God will avenge that mistreatment. The hired worker (שכר) must receive their wages "daily before sunset, because they are poor and their livelihood depends on them" (Deut 24:15). A widow (אלמנה) should not be misused or reduced to poverty along with her orphaned child (יתום) (Exod 22:22; Isa 1:17; Jer 7:6, 22:3).[26] Yet, they often were because they had no man to speak on their behalf (Isa 1:23, 10:2; Job 24:3; Ps 94:6). God, however, represents their cause (Jer 49:11; Prov 15:25; Ps 68:5, 146:9). And a resident alien (גר) must not be oppressed (Lev 19:33-34; Exod 22:21, 23:9; Deut 24:17, 27:19), because "I am the Lord your God" (Lev 19:33). While Mal 3:5 gives no specific consequences for those who break these rules, if the messenger's conduct is any indication, then the oppressors will not fare well at God's hands.

25. Athalya Brenner, ed., *Prophets and Daniel: A Feminist Companion to the Prophets*, FCB 2/8 (New York: Bloomsbury T&T Clark: 2002).

26. Weyde, *Prophecy and Teaching*, 307.

Adulterers seem to be an intermediate category, falling between sinners against needy people and sinners against God. The prohibition regarding adultery in Exod 20:14 and Deut 5:18 protects the authority of a married man over his wife, who cannot have sex with anyone but him.[27] Many passages in the Hebrew Bible give practical consequences for men who break this rule by having sex with another man's wife: the wrath of a jealous husband (Prov 6:32-35), capital punishment (Lev 20:10), and divine punishment (Jer 5:7, 29:23). Women too may be executed for adultery (Lev 20:10). A woman who is not a virgin upon marriage may be stoned to death, but a man who falsely accuses her of engaging in sex before marriage or a man who rapes her before marriage must pay a fine to her father (Deut 22:13-19). The slandered or sexually violated woman's compensation is lifelong marriage to the man who harmed her (Deut 22:28-29). A man who accuses his wife of adultery may force her to drink unclean water (Num 5:11-30); if he is wrong, however, "the man shall be free from iniquity, but the woman shall bear her iniquity" (Num 5:31). Also, a woman's vows to God may be annulled by her husband or by her father if she is single (Num 30:3-16). Malachi, therefore, maintains the establishment of masculine honor, reputation, and control, reinforced through many Torah passages. God may defend widows, but daughters and wives receive paltry divine assistance.

Just as God determines to punish those who dishonor him with defective animals, God speaks against those who question his power, specifically sorcerers, "those who swear falsely . . . and do not fear me" (Mal 3:5). The verb כשף, "to practice sorcery," rarely appears in the Hebrew Bible. Manasseh engages in the act (2 Chr 33:6), and Deuteronomy describes a sorcerer as "abhorrent to the LORD," commanding that "you must remain completely loyal to the LORD your God" (18:10, 12-13). Egypt and Babylon also have sorcerers (Exod 7:11; Dan 2:2). No punishment exists for male sorcerers, but "you shall not permit a female sorcerer to live" (Exod 22:18). Webster's Unabridged Dictionary defines sorcery as "the art, practices, or spells of a person who is supposed to exercise supernatural powers through the aid of evil spirits." The last two words of the definition may be an assumption. If a person is not a designated religious figure, like a priest, then any power that person has allegedly must be from a malevolent source. But as one of my students, a huge

27. Edward L. Greenstein, "The Exodus and History," in *The Harper Collins Study Bible, Fully Revised and Updated*, ed. Harold W. Attridge (San Francisco: HarperSanFrancisco, 2006), 118.

Harry Potter fan, pointed out years ago, sorcerers can be good people, too. Nevertheless, Malachi's condemnation of sorcerers protects clerical power, such as it is. Once the priests have been sufficiently chastened, their position will be restored against all comers. And God's rightful position will be restored as well; only he merits worship, as opposed to other gods and anyone who presumably works for them.

"Those who swear falsely" also appear to violate the commandment against improper use of the divine name (Exod 20:7; Deut 5:11). Malachi 1 emphasizes the greatness of God's name, and failure to respect that greatness will place the one who swears on God's bad side. The LXX adds "in my name" to the phrase about swearing falsely in Mal 3:5, possibly for emphasis, and David B. Freedman notes that Talmudic texts add the same phrase.[28] Even without it, however, the meaning remains basically the same: if a person promises to do something and does not, then that person has forsworn. Malachi 1:14 gives an example: "Cursed be the cheat who has a male in the flock and vows to give it, and yet sacrifices to the Lord what is blemished." Swearing falsely constitutes another honor violation, with God being the wronged party.

The last category of sinners who will face God's judgment is both the most vague and the most specific: the people who "do not fear me" (Mal 3:5). Fear of the Lord serves as a necessary prerequisite for obedience to the commandments. Whether warning against mistreating the physically disabled (Lev 19:14), stealing from others (Lev 25:17), financially exploiting the poor relatives (Lev 25:36, 43), or disrespecting the elderly (Lev 19:32), each commandment presumes "fear of God" is the reason for obeying God. Carol J. Dempsey describes Mic 6:8 as "the prophetic teaching on true religion."[29] The verse reads, "He has told you, O mortal, what is good; and what does the Lord require of you but to do justice, and to love kindness, and to walk humbly with your God?" (Mic 6:8). Compare, however, Deuteronomy's definition of religion: "So now, O Israel, what does the Lord your God require of you? Only to fear the Lord your God, to walk in all his ways, to love him, to serve the Lord your God with all your heart and with all your soul, and to keep the commandments of the Lord your God and his decrees that I am commanding you today, for your own well-being" (Deut 10:12-13). Malachi strikes a balance

28. David B. Freedman, "An Unnoted Support for a Variant to the MT of Mal 3:5," *JBL* 98 (1979): 405–06.

29. Carol J. Dempsey, "Micah," in *The Harper Collins Study Bible, Fully Revised and Updated*, ed. Harold W. Attridge (San Francisco: HarperSanFrancisco, 2006), 1247.

between both definitions, condemning those who arrogantly mistreat the poor and those who arrogantly mistreat God. The rationale for the prohibition against idolatry describes God as a jealous deity who punishes the great-grandchildren of the disobedient (Exod 20:5//Deut 5:9). Malachi reinforces this divine job description.

In his penultimate sentence on Mal 3:5, Redditt notes that "Judah was God's extended family, so the power of the father extended to the maintenance of justice and the avoidance of evil."[30] As a parental model, however, power intertwines with fear and social control. Prophetic and non-prophetic literature depicts "God as a controlling, authoritative, punishing father."[31] While the more violent image of God appears in his mandate to the messenger in Mal 3:2-3, even Mal 3:5 is not totally benign. God's judgment demands a heavy-handed return to proper order and obedience. Although some intentions behind the exercise of destructive dominance may be good (social justice), the ends may not justify the means. The violent reinforcement of patriarchal authority reappears in Malachi's final oracle. For now, Julia M. O'Brien's words serve as a fitting conclusion: "Ideological critique of the Prophetic Books calls to clear, even painful, attention just how essential the dimension of authoritarian control is to the biblical image of God the Father."[32]

30. Redditt, *Haggai, Zechariah, Malachi*, 178.

31. Julia M. O'Brien, *Challenging Prophetic Metaphor: Theology and Ideology in the Prophets* (Louisville, KY: Westminster John Knox, 2008), 82.

32. Ibid., 92.

Malachi 3:6-12

(Don't) Give Until It Hurts

Feminist biblical criticism, like modern historiography, rejects the myth of scholarly objectivity. In other words, feminist critics argue that all writers work from a particular context. As a feminist critic and a rhetorical critic who studies how language functions in different historical settings, I appreciate the freedom to be subjective regarding Mal 3:6-12; this passage gives me the most difficulty precisely because of my familiarity with it. As an African-American woman who was raised in Pentecostal churches in the 1980s, I heard this passage every Sunday for years, right before the ushers passed the collection plate. And as a teenager coming of age during the Oral Roberts, Jim Bakker, and Jimmy Swaggart controversies, I heard Mal 3 within the context of economic exploitation of the faithful and of ministerial excess masked by pious rhetoric. Quite frankly, I cannot tithe to a church as an adult, and that shapes my understanding of this text.

Intratextually, the section on tithing raises several questions. What does Mal 3:6 mean and what purpose does it serve? What is the relevance of tithes and offerings? What are the differences between them? What will the people gain if they tithe properly, according to the prophet? Intertextually, however, I find the passage problematic for reasons that I cannot separate from all those years of hearing it in church. First, if tithers' reward comes in successful farming (Mal 3:11), then the justification for tithing may be unpersuasive. Failure to rebuild the temple

Mal 3:6-12

[6]For I the LORD do not change; therefore you, O children of Jacob, have not perished. [7]Ever since the days of your ancestors you have turned aside from my statutes and have not kept them. Return to me, and I will return to you, says the LORD of hosts. But you say, "How shall we return?"

[8]Will anyone rob God? Yet you are robbing me! But you say, "How are we robbing you?" In your tithes and offerings! [9]You are cursed with a curse, for you are robbing me—the whole nation of you! [10]Bring the full tithe into the storehouse, so that there may be food in my house, and thus put me to the test, says the LORD of hosts; see if I will not open the windows of heaven for you and pour down for you an overflowing blessing. [11]I will rebuke the locust for you, so that it will not destroy the produce of your soil; and your vine in the field shall not be barren, says the LORD of hosts. [12]Then all nations will count you happy, for you will be a land of delight, says the LORD of hosts.

apparently explains crop failure in Haggai, and building initiatives should lead to abundance. If, however, the people still face poor yields, even after following one set of divinely motivated instructions, why have confidence that life will improve this time? Second, the use of Mal 3:6-12 as a prosperity gospel prooftext (faithful tithing to God guarantees wealth) creates theological difficulties.[1] Third, for women, who are so often socialized to give and give and give, Malachi's call can sound like one more oppressive and demanding male voice.

Karl M. Weyde may be a lone voice in his suggestion that Mal 3:6 belongs in the previous oracle, but his suggestion points to a problem with Mal 3:6-7: the verses do not fit within the discussion of tithing in the following verses. As Paul L. Redditt notes, "In their present context . . . vv. 6-7 form a vague introduction to the dispute over tithes."[2] Perhaps the verses act as a transition between impending judgment (Mal 3:1-5) and a call to avoid such judgment through proper tithing (Mal 3:8-12). An additional scholarly educated guess involves redaction. Specifically, Mal 3:6-7 may be the original ending to the first oracle of Mal 1:2-5, because of the reference to Jacob.[3] God loves Jacob, based on two

1. Stacy Davis, "Malachi," in *The Africana Bible: Reading Israel's Scriptures from Africa and the African Diaspora*, ed. Hugh R. Page Jr. (Minneapolis: Fortress, 2010), 213.

2. Paul L. Redditt, *Haggai, Zechariah, Malachi* (Grand Rapids, MI: Eerdmans, 1995), 178.

3. Ibid.; David L. Petersen, *Zechariah 9–14 and Malachi* (Louisville, KY: Westminster John Knox, 1995), 214.

arguments: God hates Esau and will destroy it (Mal 1:3-4), and God has not destroyed disobedient Jacob (Mal 3:6-7). As Mal 3:6 states, "For I the LORD do not change; therefore you, O children of Jacob, have not perished." Ryan E. Stokes argues that שנא (*šāna'*), "to change," should be translated as שׂנא (*śāna'*), "to hate," making the verse an even stronger conclusion to Mal 1:2-5. God does not hate Jacob; he hates only Esau. The emendation does not remove the theological difficulties of divine hatred, as Stokes points out, advising readers to "keep in mind that the world of today's professional theologian, in which God's universal love is often assumed, was not the world of Malachi's interlocutors."[4] The distinction, however, by extension suggests that accepting ancient ideas in modern times should not be done uncritically. If modern readers can reject the ancient claim that God hates a group of people, then why do some modern readers still accept the claim that humans can rob God by not tithing? Both premises appear in the same text.

When the prophet asks, "Will anyone rob God?" God says the people respond, "How are we robbing you?" (Mal 3:8). The question should not be quickly dismissed. The comparison of withholding tithes to robbing God only occurs here. As Weyde summarizes, "Disobedience to the laws of tithe is *interpreted* as robbing God,"[5] but how can a mortal rob a deity? Psalm 50, which does not reject the sacrificial system, does reject the idea that people can deprive God of material goods. God claims:

> I will not accept a bull from your house, or goats from your folds. For every wild animal of the forest is mine, the cattle on a thousand hills. I know all the birds of the air, and all that moves in the field is mine. If I were hungry, I would not tell you, for the world and all that is in it is mine. Do I eat the flesh of bulls, or drink the blood of goats? Offer to God a sacrifice of thanksgiving, and pay your vows to the Most High. (50:9-14)

Who eats animal flesh in this context? Human animals do, not God. People cannot rob God, but they can rob other people, specifically the priests and the poor, if they do not tithe.

As explained in chapter 6 on Mal 1:6–2:9, priests depend on sacrifices for their livelihood. Such sacrifices go beyond animals. Leviticus states

4. Ryan E. Stokes, "I, Yhwh, Have Not Changed? Reconsidering the Translation of Malachi 3:6; Lamentations 4:1; and Proverbs 24:21-22," *CBQ* 70 (2008): 276.

5. Karl William Weyde, *Prophecy and Teaching: Prophetic Authority, Form Problems, and the Use of Traditions in the Book of Malachi* (Berlin: de Gruyter, 2000), 330.

that priests may also eat grain offerings (2:1-10, 7:9-10). Additionally, "all tithes from the land, whether the seed from the ground or the fruit from the tree, are the LORD's; they are holy to the LORD" (Lev 27:30). By implication, such vegetarian tithes belong to the priests. Numbers 18 makes the implication explicit. The priests earn a portion of offerings, including grain, oil, wine, and "first fruits" (Num 18:9-13). Such food functions as payment for their priestly duties, and the Levites themselves must take tithes from it and pay the Aaronid priests (Num 18:21-28). Nehemiah 10 describes a similar practice; the people give tithes to the Levites, and the Levites give tithes to the temple priests (10:35-39). The system depends on every person doing their part. If people neglect the tithes or bring them sporadically, then priests and Levites may not eat well; and in the Levites' case, they must work on their farms instead of in the temple in order to support themselves and their families (Neh 13:10-14).

The poor depend on the tithe too. Deuteronomy mentions the tithe of the third year, of which not only the Levites but also "the resident aliens, the orphans, and the widows in your towns, may come and eat their fill" (Deut 14:29//26:12). Such economically vulnerable populations benefit from the more prosperous community members. The difference between tithe recipients may be due to different Torah traditions, but they share a common idea: the tithe belongs to those who cannot easily feed themselves. Insufficient sacrifices and offerings, therefore, may lead to malnutrition.

The prophet says God demands that the people "bring the full tithe into the storehouse, so that there may be food in my house," but then the prophet invites the people to test God and expect a reward (Mal 3:10). If the people tithe, then God says, "see if I will not open the windows of heaven for you and pour down for you an overflowing blessing" (Mal 3:10). The blessing depends on the people's giving.[6] What will the reward be? More food, and that will lead to more tithes.[7] While Redditt points out the symbolic blessing from heaven language, literally the blessing may be rain.[8] Malachi 3:11 supports the argument that the divine blessings will result in improved crop production, which more rain will bring:

6. Redditt, *Haggai, Zechariah, Malachi*, 180; Petersen, *Zechariah 9–14 and Malachi*, 271; Weyde, *Prophecy and Teaching*, 327, 334. In a footnote, Weyde states that the language here emphasizes "the idea of YHWH's reliability/faithfulness" more than a simple cause-effect statement: tithe and receive a blessing (2000: 334–35).

7. Davis, "Malachi," 214.

8. Redditt, *Haggai, Zechariah, Malachi*, 180; Petersen, *Zechariah 9–14 and Malachi*, 217–18; Weyde, *Prophecy and Teaching*, 335–37.

"I will rebuke the locust for you, so that it will not destroy the produce of your soil, and your vine in the field shall not be barren, says the LORD of hosts." Proper tithing will yield successful harvests, similar to the promise of fertile land, contingent upon covenant obedience, in Deut 28 and 30.[9] Additionally, the locust (אכל), or possibly caterpillar (the word literally means "devourer"), will stop eating people's produce.[10]

TRANSLATION MATTERS:

Because Mal 3:8 specifically mentions "tithes and offerings," המעשר והתרומה, there is debate regarding what tithe tradition(s) the prophet utilizes. Leviticus 27 and Deut 14 and 26 use only מעשר to describe both the tithe that belongs to the priests and Levites and the tithe that feeds the poor. In Num 18:11, the Levites receive an offering (תרומה) from the people, along with the tithe (מעשר) from which they give a tithe to the Aaronids (Num 18:26, 28). Nehemiah 10:38 states that the people will bring "our contributions" (תרומתינו) to the priests, along with the tithe (מעשר) to the Levites; then, the Levites give a tithe to the priests. Weyde thinks that tithes and offerings mean the same as "the full tithe" (כל־המעשר) in Mal 3:10. Since the phrase also appears in Deut 14:28 and 26:12, Malachi refers to that tradition, and Weyde then reads Num 18 and Neh 10 into "the full tithe" so that it also includes the tithe the priests receive from the Levites.[11] This reading seems unnecessarily convoluted. David L. Petersen takes a simpler approach by arguing that Mal 3 and Neh 10 describe the same activity.[12] In the Persian period, the people had "the general tithe and the tithe of the tithe or the tithe tax"; the first tithe goes to the local storehouse, and the second tithe to Jerusalem.[13] If Petersen is right, and the linguistic evidence does support him, then Malachi's concern about the tithe revolves around sufficient food for the priests and not the poor, similar to the complaints regarding substandard sacrifices in Mal 1. In both cases, the people give to the clergy, but not enough and not enough of the proper things.

The oracle ends joyfully: "Then all nations will count you happy, for you will be a land of delight, says the LORD of hosts" (Mal 3:12), but I view the good news suspiciously. The prophet has yet to be unconditionally cheerful, and this passage is no exception. Supposedly, if the people

9. Redditt, *Haggai, Zechariah, Malachi*, 180-81; Weyde, *Prophecy and Teaching*, 337, 339.

10. Victor Avigdor Hurowitz, "אכל in Malachi 3:11 – Caterpillar," *JBL* 121 (2002): 327–30.

11. Weyde, *Prophecy and Teaching*, 331–32.

12. Petersen, *Zechariah 9–14 and Malachi*, 215–16.

13. Ibid., 216.

just do as they are told, all will be well. But they have heard this before. Petersen sums it up: "In analysis similar to that in Haggai (e.g., Hag.1:7-11), the writer links proper human activity toward the deity with agricultural yield."[14] This suggests that failure to tithe has brought "a curse" (Mal 3:9) of drought.[15] Rebuilding the temple, according to Haggai, will end drought problems; the prophet writes, "From this day on, from the twenty-fourth day of the ninth month since the day that the foundation of the LORD's temple was laid . . . from this day on I will bless you" (Hag 2:18-19). Was this blessing somehow conditional too? If the temple has been completed, then why does drought continue to be an issue? Malachi's final oracle, even more strongly than Mal 2:17, expresses the people's frustration with obedience; their efforts seem to yield nothing. And the perceived connection between tithing and crop failure may be another example of that futility. While several generations have passed between the time of Haggai's prophecies and Malachi's oracles, the threat and reality of crop failure remain. The subpar agricultural yields may not inspire human confidence in God's character or divine willingness or ability to provide for human needs. No wonder the first question in the book of Malachi is "how have you loved us?" (Mal 1:2).

If the text presents some challenges within its biblical context, they look like nothing in comparison to the theological disaster area of Christian use of Malachi's call to tithe, particularly among African Americans. Malachi 3:10-11 has been interpreted regularly as a quid pro quo: "In African American prosperity theology, the reward is guaranteed freedom from debt (Atlanta-based pastor Creflo Dollar), a hundredfold return on your financial investment if you tithe from your *gross* income (Jakes 2000: 57, 66, 73–74), and/or the assurance that God wants the giver to be rich and to flaunt his or her wealth (Kim 1996: 19)."[16] Women ministers like Dr. Cynthia Hale make similar arguments, insisting that tithing must be an essential part of a Christian's budget.[17] In Malachi, God commands tithing, which "is a significant sign of God's Lordship in our lives. If Jesus is not Lord of all He is not Lord at all."[18] Whether a person can

14. Petersen, *Zechariah 9–14 and Malachi*, 213.

15. Weyde, *Prophecy and Teaching*, 337.

16. Davis, "Malachi," 213.

17. DebtFreedom08-02.2011.ppt; Session208-09-11.ppt; Session308-16-11.ppt (http://rayofhope.org). Accessed summer 2011.

18. ManagingYourTreasurePart210-11-11.ppt (http://rayofhope.org). Accessed summer 2011.

afford to tithe never enters the discussion; the implication is if you are poor, you cannot afford to ignore tithing because God only blesses those who bless God.[19] With stories of ministers living lavishly off the gifts of poor parishioners, however, is the "10 percent to the church" rule unequivocally a good idea?

I think not, but I do appreciate attempts to redeem the practice of tithing; at its best, tithing supports a community's poor and vulnerable members. Katie Cannon states, "A Black womanist liberation Christian ethic is a critique of all human domination in light of Black women's experience, a faith praxis that unmasks whatever threatens the well-being of the poorest women of color."[20] Such women should not be called to tithe as some type of Christian litmus test, Luke 21:1-4 notwithstanding. In that story, the widow gives more than the rich people, "for all of them have contributed out of their abundance, but she out of her poverty has put in all she had to live on" (Luke 21:4). Why is this act positive? If anything, she should be receiving tithes, according to Deuteronomy, not paying them. Fortunately, the idea of tithing as empowering as opposed to impoverishing appears to be spreading around the globe. Carlos Raúl Sosa Siliézar interprets the storehouse in Mal 3:10 as a place to provide for the needy in Guatemala that should not be equated with a local church, as is often the case in prosperity theology.[21] Lekgetho Moretsi argues that black Reformed churches in South Africa should encourage tithing as a means to create economic independence from wealthier white

19. Thomas Dexter Jakes, *The Great Investment: Balancing Faith, Family, and Finance to Build a Rich Spiritual Life* (New York: Berkley Books, 2002), 4, 19–20; T. Cedric Brown, *Show Me the Money: Malachi 3:8-11*, delivered 5 June 2005 (Washington, DC: Greater Mount Calvary Holy Church, 2005), CD-ROM.

20. Katie G. Cannon, "Roundtable Response to: Christian Ethics and Theology in Womanist Perspective," *Journal of Feminist Studies in Religion* 5, 2 (1989): 100.

21. Carlos Raúl Sosa Siliézar, "¿Ofrenda para el templo o economía solidaria? Conflicto de interpretaciones en Malaquías 3:10," *Teología y cultura* 4 (2007): 126, 128–30. Interestingly, similar arguments appear in discourse about tithing in late medieval England. While most texts insisted that tithes must be paid regardless of the clergy's worthiness, some suggested that laity need only pay tithes to reliable clergy. As Robert N. Swanson concludes, "Going even further, the expectation that relief of the poor should be one of the prime uses of tithes opened up the possibility of debate and conflict over their being granted to the ordinary clergy at all." Robert N. Swanson, "Pay Back Time? Tithes and Tithing in Late Medieval England," in *God's Bounty: The Churches and the Natural World*, ed. Peter Clarke and Tony Claydon (Suffolk: Boydell, 2010), 125–28, 131–32.

churches.[22] He concludes, "It is my conviction that if the principle of constant giving or tithing can be implemented, the financial situation of these churches will change for the better."[23] Miracle Ajah makes the same point regarding African mainline churches.[24] And Devaka Premawardhana's study of a Boston congregation of the Brazilian Universal Church of the Kingdom of God indicates that the Cape Verdean immigrants there view tithing as a source of hope. The tithers' opinion of themselves changes for the better, even if their circumstances remain the same; they have the power to help instead of always being helped, and they see their relationship with God as stronger.[25]

Even with these positive developments, Mal 3:6-12 remains a troublesome text, particularly for women today. Almost from birth, socialization encourages women to sacrifice themselves for others. In Christian traditions, such socialization gets overlaid with Scripture. As soon as Jesus heals Peter's mother-in-law, "she got up and began to serve him" (Matt 8:15). While servant/slave language appears regularly in the Bible as one way to describe divine-human relationships, women may interpret that language negatively. A theologian friend of mine recalls almost walking out of a church service after hearing Luke 17:9-10: "Do you thank the slave for doing what was commanded? So you also, when you have done all that you were ordered to do, say, 'We are worthless slaves; we have done only what we ought to have done!'" She noted that for women, whose responsibilities often seem endless, the last thing they need to hear is God's demand for additional work, to which the acceptable response must be obedient self-abasement. Tithing language can strike the same sharp note: give or be cursed as thieves.

Bishop Vashti McKenzie, the first woman bishop of the African Methodist Episcopal Church, posted a prayer during the 2012 Lenten season that offers a more life-giving approach to the act of giving: "May the spirit of generosity overcome us and lead us to give ourselves, our souls and bodies as a *reasonable* sacrifice today. . . . Empower us to . . . give

22. Lekgetho Moretsi, "Tithing: An Evaluation of the Biblical Background," *In Die Skriflig* 43 (2009): 398–99.

23. Ibid., 409.

24. Miracle Ajah, "Tithing in Ugarit and the Pentateuch: Possible Implications for Africa," *Scriptura* 91 (2006): 31, 39–40.

25. Devaka Premawardhana, "Transformational Tithing: Sacrifice and Reciprocity in a Neo-Pentecostal Church," *Nova Religio: The Journal of Alternative and Emergent Religions* 15 (2012): 87, 90–91, 93, 97, 100.

our love without seeking reciprocity and to give our treasure to undergird our work."[26] The use of "reasonable" presents a gentleness and openness often neglected in prosperity theology and in Mal 3 itself, in which people give in order to get.

When Giving Hurts: On Tithing from Precarity

Sometimes I count myself among the lost generation of academics—one among many who found that, in the years of the Great Recession, jobs in my chosen field of religious studies simply evaporated, never to return. Sarah Kendzior aptly described it as "The Job Market Recovery That Never Came."[27] The nonexistent recovery was true not only for would-be professors but in sector after sector, for job after job. Dreams we had thought would be merely deferred eventually shriveled into dreams denied. The situation really was a job market version of the Rapture, where a select few were whisked into the relative—if illusory and tenuous—safety of the academy, while the rest of us were left behind to fend for ourselves and make sense of the brokenness.

So goes the reality of graduating at the wrong time, and particularly into the humanities. In the wake of being stranded, we scrambled to make other plans: to stay financially afloat and professionally relevant while looking for meaningful, dignified work of any kind (really!) that would pay the rent and keep food on the table; to shield our families from the worst of our struggles so that they would have a little cushion against shame and worry. The big-ticket education for which we had sacrificed so much and taken on debt eventually became more liability than asset. What was our worth if not measured out in course evaluations, conference talks, and publications?

At my lowest point of this period, I was receiving government assistance and taking on any odd jobs that came my way just to patch through. My meager savings—already decimated after a series of cross-country moves where I "did what I was supposed to do" by "paying my dues" and "following the job"—dwindled as the unemployment clock

26. Vashti Murphy McKenzie, "Live to Give" *Praycation: with Bishop Vashti Murphy McKenzie* (blog), 23 March 2012, www.vashtimckenzie.blogspot.com/2012_03_01_archive.html.

27. Sarah Kendzior, "The Job Market Recovery That Never Came," *The Chronicle of Higher Education*, 26 Sept 2014, https://chroniclevitae.com/news/724-the-job-market-recovery-that-never-came.

ticked down, and I lived in constant dread terror that I might be evicted one day if nothing came through. The margin for error was razor-thin, and juggling the obligations, needs, and lacks was beyond stressful.[28] The balance often felt so fragile that a whisper would have undone an existence that felt as if it were being held together by little more than staples and duct tape. When I encountered homeless women and men on the street and saw the starkness of their absolute need, even relative to my own economic insecurity, I was sometimes ashamed of my almost involuntary prayer: Please, God, don't let me end up like that. I want to get through this, and I need the strength and hope to persist. What a sorry, imperfect, desperate prayer.

To belong to the precariat is a funny thing; no one would choose to be a part of it, but the term does name honestly enough the economic instability, exploitation, and disenfranchisement exacerbated by a sense of powerlessness to overcome it all, at least for oneself, if not also for others. I think about all these things as I go through my own hardships and see the struggles that others suffer as well. For instance, I have watched long-standing parishes merge with nearby ones or close because the demographics have shifted and their home communities can no longer support them adequately. I currently belong to a historic parish that has a deep sense of rootedness and mission, but it is struggling financially. In the last decade, the parish made the difficult decision to close its K–8 school because the school did not have enough students and families nearby to sustain it any longer. In the last year, this same church has seen the diocesan contribution it is expected to raise nearly double, and this obligation hampers the parish from making other commitments that it would like. The promise of making all things new (Rev 21:5) does not diminish the pain of loss or make tough decisions any easier.

In the same vein, Generation Student Debt has to square its obligations and dreams with reality and hard choices, all while grieving what we had thought was in our grasp but what we will likely never attain. While we recognize the value and necessity of the tithing, it feels onerous. Keeping Malachi's warnings in mind (Mal 3:6-12), how can we give freely and selflessly when we ourselves are in need or—worse yet—in crisis?

28. KillerGibsons, "Why I Make Terrible Decisions, or poverty thoughts," *Killermartinis* blog (22 Oct 2013), http://killermartinis.kinja.com/why-i-make-terrible-decisions-or-poverty-thoughts-1450123558.

God knows, this is what precarity feels like. Giving from a state of want and brokenness fosters resentment and a hardened heart. Surely, if we had more to give, we could give more freely, and with a more open and generous heart.

Keeping in mind that not all suffering is redemptive, the impulse and expectation of sacrifice conflicts with our fundamental will to live and the (feminist, liberative) idea that God wants our flourishing—flourishing, yes, but surely not at extreme and unreasonable cost. Is this preferential option for the vulnerable and marginalized we keep talking about actually true and meaningful, or have we just been talking a good game to make ourselves feel better about accepting the intractability of poverty in a system structured to wreak economic violence? If we ask for help, are we in fact robbing God, as Malachi suggests? When can we acceptably ask for help? When can we legitimately claim that our need is real? When can we receive that help with grace? Above all, when and how can we balance these obligations to God and community with the necessity of self-care?

Pairing Malachi's call with the story of the widow's mite (Mark 12:41-44; Luke 21:1-4) would imply that detachment from material possessions—even at cost to oneself—and radical dependence on God would bring blessings and favors. In the real world, though, which values independence and self-reliance, the externally imposed humiliation of unemployment or food stamps and the looming threat of eviction feel like the complete opposite. Instead of blessedness and favor, living in and from precarity feels like an utter curse. As numerous studies have shown, precarity makes it difficult to plan and live a normal life.[29] Living from paycheck to paycheck or even less shows precarity for what it is: a leech, literally sucking and draining life out.

All of us are the stewards of the lives we are given. In this light, we have to care for ourselves in order to make it more possible to care for others. As we consider tithing—whether and when to give at all, as well as why and how much—we must ask ourselves whether we are giving due weight to meeting both human needs and spiritual concerns. Even when in a situation of precarity—

29. For example, see Anandi Mani et al., "Poverty Impedes Cognitive Function," *Science* 341, no. 6149 (30 Aug 2013): 976–80; and Dean Spears, "Economic Decision-Making in Poverty Depletes Cognitive Control," unpublished manuscript, Princeton University, Princeton, NJ (2010), https://www.princeton.edu/chw/events_archive/repository/Spears120110/Spears120110.pdf.

defined by its lack and instability, and riddled with fear and disappointment—we want to be able to give and receive in a way that still makes space for gratitude, connection, and real life. Tithing is not exempt from the mandate to choose life (Deut 30:15-20), so our challenge is to find ways to do it that are sustainable and promote flourishing rather than depletion.

Rachel A. R. Bundang, PhD

Malachi 3:13–4:3

Warning: God Will Reign

Unlike the previous passages, monologue, not dialogue, describes Malachi's last oracle. Additional complaints about God's injustice expand their initial protest in Mal 2:17, and then the textual style changes. After a narrative transition in Mal 3:16, God gets the last word. He defends his honor and masculine role as "the man" by insisting that divine retribution will happen on a future day. An old rationale justifies a new argument: God continues to insist upon his rank as "father" and "master" (Mal 1:6). His dominance may be delayed but cannot be denied.

The "harsh words" (Mal 3:13) echo the wearisome words in Mal 2:17. In the earlier oracle, the speakers complain that God takes pleasure in evildoers. Here, they expand that argument, concluding that "it is vain to serve God. What do we profit by keeping his command or by going about as mourners before the Lord of hosts?" (Mal 3:14). Since the wicked flourish, the righteous feel their works bear no fruit, that they do not profit or prosper more than the wicked. Once again, the people question divine retribution.[1] Paul L. Redditt concludes, "The prophet

1. Paul L. Redditt, *Haggai, Zechariah, Malachi* (Grand Rapids, MI: Eerdmans, 1995), 182; David L. Petersen, *Zechariah 9–14 and Malachi* (Louisville, KY: Westminster John Knox, 1995), 221.

Mal 3:13–4:3

[13]You have spoken harsh words
against me, says the LORD. Yet you say,
"How have we spoken against you?"
[14]You have said, "It is vain to serve
God. What do we profit by keeping his
command or by going about as mourn-
ers before the LORD of hosts? [15]Now we
count the arrogant happy; evildoers not
only prosper, but when they put God to
the test they escape."

[16]Then those who revered the LORD
spoke with one another. The LORD took
note and listened, and a book of re-
membrance was written before him of
those who revered the LORD and thought
on his name. [17]They shall be mine, says
the LORD of hosts, my special posses-
sion on the day when I act, and I will
spare them as parents spare their chil-
dren who serve them. [18]Then once
more you shall see the difference be-
tween the righteous and the wicked,
between one who serves God and one
who does not serve him.

[4:1]See, the day is coming, burning
like an oven, when all the arrogant and
all evildoers will be stubble; the day
that comes shall burn them up, says
the LORD of hosts, so that it will leave
them neither root nor branch. [2]But for
you who revere my name the sun of
righteousness shall rise, with healing
in its wings. You shall go out leaping
like calves from the stall. [3]And you shall
tread down the wicked, for they will be
ashes under the soles of your feet, on
the day when I act, says the LORD of
hosts.

laid the blame on the people and the priests for their moral and ritual failures; the people blamed God and concluded that he would not deliver."[2] Either way, each side challenges the other's masculine identity. God should be the powerful, protective father, but instead God appears impotent, and the priests should be obedient, loyal sons, but instead they appear rebellious. Malachi describes an angst-ridden relationship that the prophet's words have not improved. David L. Petersen writes, "One senses that the inability of these diatribes to effect significant change in the verbal behavior of Judean Yahwists makes this final pericope so different."[3] Since God's warning about the messenger in Mal 3:1-4 apparently falls on deaf ears,[4] God changes his audience to "those who revered the LORD" (Mal 3:16).

When, however, does God begin speaking only to his supporters? Petersen suggests that the shift begins in Mal 3:16 when God listens in on their conversation. Karl W. Weyde takes a different approach. Weyde ar-

2. Redditt, *Haggai, Zechariah, Malachi*, 182.

3. Petersen, *Zechariah 9–14 and Malachi*, 220.

4. Ibid.

gues that the complainers in Mal 3:14 are identical to those in 3:16, but they are not identical to the complainers in Mal 2:17. Weyde claims that those protesting in Mal 2:17ff. disobey God, but the dissenters in Mal 3:14-15 follow "his command."[5] Petersen has the stronger argument. Weyde accurately notes that Mal 3:16 "marks a decisive turning point in YHWH's relationship to the addressees."[6] But that does not mean that the speakers in that verse are the same speakers in the previous two verses. Since Mal 2:17 and 3:14-15 make the same argument, the words probably come from the same group. Also, while the prophet makes accusations of disobedience, these accusations have been contested (Mal 1:6-7, 2:17, 3:7-8, 13). If you think that God is not keeping his end of the covenant, then why bother following the rules at all? From that perspective, the actions described in the text are more passive resistance than direct disobedience. Finally, Weyde states that, in Mal 3:16, the speakers from Mal 3:14-15 have changed "*their* attitude to YHWH; they have returned to him."[7] Perhaps, but without any clear textual evidence, the statement lacks support. And if Weyde is right that Mal 3:16 introduces a shift in the text, "then those who revered the Lord" appear to be a different group from the second-person plural group of priests with whom the prophet has previously interacted. This new and different group will receive God's favor.

God identifies the chosen ones in a manner similar to Santa Claus: by reading "a book of remembrance" (Mal 3:16). Like Santa, who makes a list and checks it twice, an unknown writer in God's presence lists the names of the people who fear (ירא) God. The NRSV translates ירא as "revered," but fear has more theological weight in this context. Deuteronomy 10:12 states, "So now, O Israel, what does the Lord your God require of you? Only to fear [ירא] the Lord your God, to walk in all his ways, to love him, to serve the Lord your God with all your heart and with all your soul." Based on the theory of divine retribution, fearing God leads to obeying God, which opens the door to divine rewards. For this reason, scholars have focused more attention on the book of remembrance itself than on the people listed within it. Like Santa's list, however, Malachi's book allows God to reward the worthy.[8] Redditt notes that

5. Karl William Weyde, *Prophecy and Teaching: Prophetic Authority, Form Problems, and the Use of Traditions in the Book of Malachi* (Berlin: Walter de Gruyter, 2000), 359, 383, 386.

6. Ibid., 358.

7. Ibid., 384–85.

8. Petersen, *Zechariah 9–14 and Malachi*, 222–23.

Exod 32:32-33, Ps 69:28, and Dan 12:1 mention a book where the names of the righteous appear.[9] While God writes directly in Exodus, an unidentified scribe records the names in Psalms and Daniel. The righteous in Malachi will receive more than gifts under a tree; instead, "they shall be mine, says the LORD of hosts, my special possession on the day when I act, and I will spare them as parents spare their children who serve them" (Mal 3:17).

God's possession of the righteous defends God's honor. Malachi 3:17 troubles Petersen, who writes as follows: "YHWH will act toward his special possession as does a father toward his son who *serves* him. This simile is odd. . . . The imagery is something other than 'normal' paternal affection."[10] In Malachi's patriarchal context, the verse makes perfect sense. Since the second oracle, God has complained about his male children's disrespect. God longs to be treated like a father, to be honored and obeyed. Petersen claims in a footnote that "though the vocabulary of father and son occurs in Malachi 1:6, the issue is different."[11] For him, Mal 1 describes an example of filial disobedience, while Mal 3 describes filial obedience. The issue, however, may be the same. In contrast to the priests who fail to give God his due, the righteous who fear God like good sons will avoid punishment. The idea that sons should obey fathers is typical in the biblical world. According to Deut 21:18-21, parents may have their disobedient son stoned. Children who curse their parents may be executed as well (Lev 20:9//Exod 21:17). The parable in Matt 21:28-32 praises the son who eventually fulfills his father's order. Such texts need not preclude parent-child affection, but they do suggest a contingency that may be more realistic than modern claims of unconditional parental love.[12] Excluding the parental imagery, biblical precedent exists for God's claim to care only for the obedient, according to Exod 19:5 and Deut 7:6 and 14:2.[13] What is new, according to Weyde, is the limiting of God's chosen people to those who fear God.[14]

9. Redditt, *Haggai, Zechariah, Malachi*, 183; Ps 87:6 also describes God writing in a book, but the book is not limited to the names of the righteous.

10. Petersen, *Zechariah 9–14 and Malachi*, 223–24.

11. Ibid., 223, n. 99.

12. One of the best and funniest recent examples of a parent who loves their child and still wishes they would follow instructions appears in Adam Mansbach and Ricardo Cortes's *Go the Fuck to Sleep* (Brooklyn, NY: Akashic Books, 2011).

13. Weyde, *Prophecy and Teaching*, 363–64. Weyde also points out Ps 103:13, which links God's paternal compassion to human reverence.

14. Ibid., 364

The date in Malachi of God's retributive activity remains unknown, but the prophet describes the day as a time of fiery retribution. Divine retribution and eschatology now share a space, and Mal 4:1 "marks a link between late prophecy and apocalyptic."[15] The day itself, "burning like an oven," will incinerate "all the arrogant and all evildoers" (Mal 4:1). Petersen notes that "unlike the fire for smelting (Mal. 3:2-3), this oven, which presumably refers to the earthenware oven used for cooking, produces a kind of heat that this author construes as essentially destructive."[16] As with the refiner's fire examined earlier, the fire in Mal 4:1 may not be life-giving, either. The purification process in Mal 3 results in significant pain for the Levites. But they will survive, unlike the wicked in Mal 4:1, who will then have "neither root nor branch."

The long-suffering righteous will get to live out a conquest fantasy. Almost like a speaker at a pep rally, God describes a literal crushing of the enemy's remains: "But for you who revere my name the sun of righteousness shall rise, with healing in its wings. You shall go out leaping like calves from the stall. And you shall tread down the wicked, for they will be ashes under the soles of your feet" (Mal 4:2-3). While the heat of fire has a negative connotation, the sun does not. Instead, the sun represents restoration.[17] Now restored to God, the righteous display their freedom by crushing the remains of the wicked. Hélène Koehl-Krebs argues that Mal 4:2 parallels the anti-Edom oracle in Mal 1:2-5. She argues that the name of Edom's god, Qošh, sounds similar to *qăsh*, the Hebrew word for "stubble." As the sun, YHWH will burn up all stubble, including Edom and Qošh. Additionally, the same root appears in Mal 1:4, in which Edom will not be able to build (בנה), and in Mal 3:15, in which evildoers seem to "prosper" (בנה). Also, just as Edom is wicked (רשעה) (Mal 1:4), so are evildoers (עשי רשעה) (Mal 3:15). Koehl-Krebs notes that later rabbinic literature describes the sun of righteousness as a tool against Edom; one sign of the end times will be Edom's

15. Ibid., 385, 365.

16. Petersen, *Zechariah 9–14 and Malachi*, 224.

17. Redditt, *Haggai, Zechariah, Malachi*, 184; Petersen, *Zechariah 9–14 and Malachi*, 225–26; Weyde, *Prophecy and Teaching*, 375–76. Dale C. Allison, Jr. observes that early Christian writers connected "the sun of righteousness" to Jesus' healing powers. Dale C. Allison, Jr., "Healing in the Wings of His Garment: The Synoptics and Malachi 4.2," in *The Word Leaps the Gap: Essays on Scripture and Theology in Honor of Richard B. Hayes*, eds. J. Ross Wagner, C. Kavin Rowe & A. Katherine Grieb (Grand Rapids, MI: Eerdmans, 2008), 132–46.

destruction.[18] Her careful use of intertextuality actually brings the oracles full circle. If the priests' first question according to God is, "How have you loved us?" (Mal 1:2), then God's final answer is this: if you behave, then you may walk on the ashes of your enemies. God remains the ultimate warrior, allowing lesser fighters to participate in a victory dance.

Feminist readers, however, may not feel like celebrating. Writing for this volume as a reader and scholar of Malachi, I began to feel a strong sense of restlessness as I approached the final oracle. I initially mistook the feeling for the more common anxiety one experiences toward the end of a project—a combination of impatience and fatigue. What I actually felt, however, was boredom. After slogging through verse after verse of patriarchal imagery, I grew tired of hearing a God repeatedly trying to prove himself as "the man" to his increasingly unimpressed male followers. The circular argumentation and its predictability grated on my nerves. A scene from the film *Titanic* expresses a similar sentiment. After a formal dinner, Rose informs Jack that the men will soon leave to drink brandy in the smoking room; she comments sarcastically, "Now they'll retreat into a cloud of smoke and congratulate each other on being masters of the universe."[19] The divine promises made to the obedient followers seem like that cloud of smoke. Who cares that the righteous get to step on the wicked?

Perhaps this entire commentary should have come with a warning label: these prophets may increase feelings of irritation in the reader, followed quickly and closely by apathy. Julia M. O'Brien concludes that in Mal 3, "the restoration of the proper relationship between Yahweh and Israel is envisioned as a return to the proper hierarchy of the family."[20] Therefore, those who support more egalitarian social models will find Malachi a problematic text. O'Brien notes that her view of Malachi softened somewhat between March and November 1995 due to positive changes in her own life. Yet, she still insisted that Malachi's "heavy-

18. Hélène Koehl-Krebs, "L'intertextualité comme méthode d'investigation du texte biblique: L'exemple de Malachie 3,20," *BN* 121 (2004): 61–76.

19. *Titanic*, Dir. James Cameron, Perf. Leonardo DiCaprio, Kate Winslet, Paramount Pictures and Twentieth Century Fox, 1997.

20. Julia M. O'Brien, *Challenging Prophetic Metaphor: Theology and Ideology in the Prophets* (Louisville, KY: Westminster John Knox, 2008), 86.

handed argument collapses under its own weight."[21] Nearing the book's end brings a sense of relief—finally readers can extricate themselves from the web of authoritarian bluster and complaint. The prophet claims that the people have wearied God; the converse is true, too.

21. Julia M. O'Brien, "On Saying 'No' to a Prophet," in *Prophets and Daniel: A Feminist Companion to the Prophets*, ed. Athalya Brenner, FCB 2/8 (Sheffield: Sheffield Academic, 2001), 211.

Malachi 4:4-6

Who Has the Last Word?

The text appears suddenly and abruptly after the fiery description of the day of the Lord ends, unexpectedly invoking Moses and Elijah. To this point, the prophet only mentioned men from Genesis—Jacob, Esau, Levi, and Judah—although Exodus, Leviticus, and Numbers also describe the covenant with Levi. Malachi's conclusion, therefore, raises three primary questions. Is it original to the book or a redaction? Does the passage have any connection to the rest of Malachi or other parts of the Hebrew Bible? And why has Elijah appeared? No scholarly consensus exists regarding the first two questions, but a redactor probably added Mal 4:4-6 as a conclusion to the book while making allusions to the larger canon of the law and the prophets. Elijah returns to restore the ideal patriarchal familial relationships for which the original author of Malachi longed, in preparation for the end times.

Whether the end of Malachi comes from a redactor remains debatable, but the book's final three verses are most likely a later addition. Paul Redditt and Karl W. Weyde argue in favor of a redactor. Caryn A. Reeder and Fanie Snyman concur.[1] Elie Assis remains agnostic, stating that "these

1. Paul L. Redditt, *Haggai, Zechariah, Malachi* (Grand Rapids, MI: Eerdmans, 1995), 185; Karl William Weyde, *Prophecy and Teaching: Prophetic Authority, Form Problems, and the Use of Traditions in the Book of Malachi* (Berlin: Walter de Gruyter, 2000), 389; Caryn A. Reeder, "Malachi 3:24 and the Eschatological Restoration of the 'Family,'" *CBQ* 69 (2007): 697; Fanie Snyman, "Malachi 4:4-6 (Heb 3:22-24) as a point of convergence in

Malachi 4:4-6

4Remember the teaching of my servant Moses, the statutes and ordinances that I commanded him at Horeb for all Israel.

5Lo, I will send you the prophet Elijah before the great and terrible day of the LORD comes. 6He will turn the hearts of parents to their children and the hearts of children to their parents, so that I will not come and strike the land with a curse.

verses were written from the outset as the closing to the book of Malachi," but he doesn't say by whom; he simply calls the author a prophet.[2] Similarly, David L. Petersen writes, "Whether the author is the same as the one responsible for either the primary or secondary material in the dialogues is impossible to determine."[3] A footnote to that sentence, however, reads as follows: "The most compelling argument for a different author is that v. 23 [4:5] attempts to specify the identity of the messenger identified in Mal. 3:1"; and Petersen later concludes that the author of the book's end did not write the rest of the book.[4] Additionally, the book's conclusion differs in tone and style from the preceding chapters. The constant references to "the LORD" or "the LORD of Hosts" (twenty-three in Mal 1:2–4:3, the book's six oracles) cease. The dialogical/monological structure of the oracles disappears as well. God speaks, but he identifies himself indirectly and does not identify his audience. Finally, many minor prophetic books end with the phrase "says the LORD [of hosts]" (Amos 9:15; Zeph 3:20; Hag 2:23). So, Mal 4:3 easily could have been the book's original ending. Why add another conclusion?

Perhaps because Malachi's redacted verses finish the first two sections of the canon. The Deuteronomic language, such as referring to Sinai as Horeb—the preferred word in Deuteronomy—and the mention of Elijah suggest that Malachi ends both the law and the prophets.[5] Going a step further, Snyman argues that Malachi's new conclusion connects the pro-

---

the Old Testament or Hebrew Bible: A Consideration of the intra and intertextual relationships," *HTS Teologiese Studies/Theological Studies* 68 (2012): n.p.

2. Elie Assis, "Moses, Elijah and the Messianic Hope: A New Reading of Malachi 3,22–24," *ZAW* 123 (2011): 209.

3. David L. Petersen, *Zechariah 9–14 and Malachi* (Louisville, KY: Westminster John Knox, 1995), 228.

4. Ibid., 228, 232.

5. S. Dean McBride Jr., "Deuteronomy," in *The Harper Collins Study Bible, Fully Revised and Updated*, ed. Harold W. Attridge (San Francisco: HarperSanFrancisco,

phetic canon to the writings as well as the Torah; the call to "remember the teachings of my servant Moses" (Mal 4:4) repeats itself in Ps 1:2, in which happy people find "their delight. . . . in the law of the LORD."[6] At minimum, Malachi serves as a fitting conclusion to the prophetic canon, in which several books call for obedience to the Torah. The first commandments of the Torah demand fidelity to God, often shown through compassion to others (Isa 57; Jer 7; Ezek 7; Hos 4; Amos 5; Micah 2; Zeph 1; Hag 1).

Moses' appearance in the conclusion seems surprising but understandable. As the recipient of the Torah and a Levite, his presence in a text concerned primarily about obedience and disobedience and appropriate Levitical behavior makes sense. If following the covenant determines a person's reward or punishment on the day of the Lord, knowing the rules matters. Malachi's author wrote from a priestly perspective, calling for the priests to urge the people to follow "statutes and ordinances" regarding sacrifice and tithing (Mal 4:4). Whoever wrote the first verse in the revised conclusion maintained that perspective. Petersen notes, however, that "there is no direct syntactic link between vv. 22 and 23 [4-5]."[7] Therefore, Elijah's appearance seems surprising and puzzling.

Malachi 4:5 states that Elijah will arrive "before the great and terrible day of the LORD comes." Because of the prophet's previous activity and reputation, Elijah can act as an eschatological messenger. Loyal only to the "God of Abraham, Isaac, and Israel," Elijah says to God at the conclusion of his conflict with the priests of Baal that "I am your servant, and that I have done all these things at your bidding" (1 Kgs 18:36). He predicts the beginning and end of a drought and raises a child from the dead (1 Kgs 17–18). And like Moses, he encounters God at Mount Horeb (1 Kgs 19:8-18). Unlike Moses, who died at the edge of the Promised Land, Elijah enters heaven alive, in a fiery chariot. Therefore, he can return to help the people.[8] Bernard Gosse notes the parallels between Moses and Elijah, arguing that both follow the God of the patriarchs. As Moses establishes the covenant, Elijah can reinforce and restore the covenant before the end of time.[9]

2006), 257; Redditt, *Haggai, Zechariah, Malachi*, 185; Petersen, *Zechariah 9–14 and Malachi*, 228, 233.

6. Snyman, "Malachi 4:4-6 as a point of convergence," n.p.

7. Petersen, *Zechariah 9–14 and Malachi*, 229.

8. Ibid., 230; Weyde, *Prophecy and Teaching*, 392.

9. Bernard Gosse, "Abraham, Isaac et Jacob, Moise et Joseu, Elie et Elisee et L'Unification du Corpus Biblique," *EstBib* 58 (2000): 513–26.

Elijah also appears to be the "messenger of the covenant" (Mal 3:1) that the prophet mentions earlier in Malachi.[10] Weyde expresses skepticism regarding this possibility, since he thinks the tasks of the two messengers differ: the unnamed man in Mal 3:1 reforms the Levites, while Elijah restores familial relations.[11] Yet Petersen notes a linguistic parallel between Mal 3:1 and 4:5; God *sends* someone in both verses.[12] And the jobs of the two messengers share similarities. Both will restore people to God by reforming their bad behavior. Assis notes a connection between Mal 1:6 and 4:6. God complains about a disobedient child, so he will send Elijah to rectify the matter. Additionally, Elijah will enable the people to "return to . . . the LORD of hosts."[13] Reeder makes a similar argument, claiming that Elijah will restore the Israelites to their ancestors' earlier ways of properly acknowledging God. She rejects the idea that Elijah brings the children back to God their father, because "fathers" is plural in Mal 4:6, and "according to Mal 2:10, God is the *one* father of all Israel."[14] But Assis notes that Mal 1:6 refers to God in the plural; "master" in the NRSV is a plural form of *adon*.[15] Therefore, Elijah's purpose can be the restoration of disobedient Israelites to God their father.

This objective fits perfectly with Malachi's complaints throughout the book about the people's lack of respect for the divine shown through improper sacrifices, violation of oaths, and failure to tithe, to name three examples. Elijah will clean up the entire community, beginning with the clergy (Mal 3:1-4) and then the laity (Mal 4:6). God wants the honor and respect to which he, as father and master, is entitled (Mal 1:6). Elijah will give God back his status as paterfamilias, and sons will again obey and serve their father "before the great and terrible day of the LORD comes" (Mal 4:5). Just as the marriage metaphor described divine-human relations in preexilic and exilic prophetic texts, the parent-child metaphor serves the same purpose in Malachi.

The metaphor, however, does not bring comfort. Whoever added the ending of Malachi understood the rage lying just below the surface of

10. In the New Testament, Elijah and the covenant messenger become John the Baptist (Matt 11:14; Luke 1:16-17); see also Matthew Black, "The messenger, the Lord, and the Coming Judgement in the Reception History of Malachi 3," *NTS* 53 (2007): 1–16.

11. Weyde, *Prophecy and Teaching*, 392–93.

12. Petersen, *Zechariah 9–14 and Malachi*, 230.

13. Assis, "Moses, Elijah, and the Messianic Hope," 213.

14. Reeder, "Eschatological Restoration of the 'Family,'" 703; 696–97.

15. Assis, "Moses, Elijah, and the Messianic Hope," 214.

the text. Curses or threats thereof appear (Mal 1:14, 2:2, 3:9), along with violent imagery, designed to force the recalcitrant into submission (Mal 2:3, 3:3, 4:1, 4:3). The book begins with the planned destruction of Edom as a sign of God's "love" and ends with the planned restoration of the people, lest God curse them.[16] Even Malachi's original ending contains violence; the righteous walk all over the wicked people's ashes (Mal 4:3). Julia M. O'Brien makes the following statement about the prophetic text: "The book of Malachi argues that you will feel God's love if you behave. It defines the goal of life as knowing your place and staying there. To comply with Malachi is to comply with universal expectations, gender hierarchies, and physical punishment as justified, and it predicates abusive language as divine will."[17] Although O'Brien's assessment of the language softens with time, she "still found Malachi harsh."[18]

And yet, just like hope left in Pandora's box and at the end of Haggai, Malachi's seemingly overwhelming supply of patriarchal "gifts" conceals one piece of hope at the bottom of the pile. A sociologist colleague of mine, during a conversation about Malachi with gender and women's studies faculty, asked me how the book ends. Did the people accept the prophet's critique and change their ways? Immediately, I answered no—Malachi is open-ended. The book's final move to eschatology leaves the question of the people's alleged bad behavior unanswered and unresolved. They did not simply comply, and today's readers need not do so either. In the synagogue, the Torah reader repeats Mal 4:5 after Mal 4:6, "so that," as O'Brien notes, "the book will not leave you cursed."[19] Also, the last words in the dialogue in Mal 3:15 belong to the still skeptical people, and that may be a sign of hope. Malachi's nasty rhetoric need not be the final word. Therefore, my final response to Malachi echoes the words of the people to Jeremiah in Egypt: "As for the word that you have spoken to us in the name of the Lord, we are not going to listen to you" (Jer 44:16).

16. Julia M. O'Brien, "On Saying 'No' to a Prophet," in *Prophets and Daniel: A Feminist Companion to the Prophets*, ed. Athalya Brenner, FCB 2/8 (Sheffield: Sheffield Academic, 2001), 207–08.

17. Ibid., 208.

18. Ibid., 211.

19. Ibid., 208.

Afterword

A Feminist Rhetorical Critical Comment

Writing a feminist commentary, especially about deeply masculinist texts like Haggai and Malachi, contributes to scholarship in general and feminist scholarship and causes in particular. J. David Hester Amador accuses feminist biblical scholars of being writers but not activists, allowing the former occupation to subsume the latter.[1] As a teacher of the prophets at a Catholic women's college, I resist this binary; scholarship enables me to introduce my students to the joys and challenges of biblical interpretation. It also helps give them the skills they need and the desire to ask hard questions about their own lives as young adult women and about their futures. I find teaching this class to be the most exhilarating and exhausting work I have ever done. Writing and speaking certainly are forms of feminist activism in my particular context, and it is with that belief in mind that I present this work.

As a rhetorical critic, I know that readers (happily) have minds of their own, and I do not control their reception of my efforts. Therefore, the words of 2 Maccabees serve as my conclusion: "If it is well told and to the point, that is what I myself desired; if it is poorly done or mediocre, that was the best I could do" (2 Macc 15:38).

1. J. David Hester Amador, "Feminist Biblical Hermeneutics: A Failure of Theoretical Nerve," *JAAR* 66 (1998): 39–57.

Haggai Works Cited

Abbott, Jacob. *History of Cyrus the Great*. New York: Harper & Brothers Publishers, 1850.

Assis, Elie. "Composition, Rhetoric and Theology in Haggai 1:1-11." *JHebS* 7 (2007): 2–14.

———. "A Disputed Temple (Haggai 2, 1-9)." *ZAW* 120 (2008): 582–96.

———. "To Build or Not to Build: A Dispute between Haggai and His People (Hag 1)." *ZAW* 119 (2007): 514–27.

Brown, Francis, S. R. Driver, and Charles A. Briggs. *A Hebrew and English Lexicon of the Old Testament*. Peabody, MA: Hendrickson, 1994.

Bedford, Peter Ross. "Discerning the Time: Haggai, Zechariah, and the 'Delay' in the Rebuilding of the Jerusalem Temple." In *The Pitcher Is Broken: Memorial Essays for Gösta W. Ahlström*. Edited by Steven W. Holloway and Lowell K. Handy, 71–94. Sheffield: Sheffield Academic, 1995.

Benjamin, Samuel G. W. *Persia*. London: T. Fisher Unwin, 1920.

Boda, Mark J. "Haggai: Master Rhetorician." *TynBul* 51 (2000): 295–304.

———. "Majoring on the Minors: Recent Research on Haggai and Zechariah." *CurBR* 2 (2003): 33–68.

Carroll, John T. "Eschatology." In *Eerdmans Dictionary of the Bible*. Edited by David Noel Freedman, Allen C. Myers, and Astrid B. Beck, 420–22. Grand Rapids, MI: Eerdmans, 2000.

Clark, David J. "Problems in Haggai 2.15-19." *BT* 34 (1983): 432–39.

Connell, Raewyn W. *Masculinities*. 2nd ed. Berkeley: University of California Press, 2005.

Davidson, Steed Verynl. "Haggai." In *The Peoples' Bible*. Edited by Curtiss Paul DeYoung, Wilda C. Gafney, Leticia A. Guardiola-Saenz, George "Tink" Tinker, and Frank M. Yamada, 1095–98. Minneapolis, MN: Fortress, 2009.

Dubbink, Joep. "Ähnlich Und Doch Ganz Anders: Priester Und Propheten Über Die Begriffe *Heilig* Und *Unrein*." *Communio Viatorum* 50 (2008): 6–19.

Fewell, Danna Nolan. "Feminist Criticism." In *To Each Its Own Meaning: An Introduction to Biblical Criticisms and Their Applications*. Edited by Steven L. McKenzie and Stephen R. Haynes, 268–82. Rev. and exp. ed. Louisville, KY: Westminster John Knox, 1999.

Fontaine, Carole R. "The Abusive Bible: On the Use of Feminist Method in Pastoral Contexts." In *A Feminist Companion to Reading the Bible: Approaches, Methods and Strategies*. Edited by Athalya Brenner and Carole Fontaine, 84–113. Sheffield: Sheffield Academic, 1997.

Geertz, Clifford. *The Interpretation of Cultures: Selected Essays*. New York: Basic Books, 1973.

Goswell, Greg. "The Fate and Future of Zerubbabel in the Prophecy of Haggai." *Bib* 91 (2010): 77–90.

Hildebrand, David R.. "Temple Ritual: A Paradigm for Moral Holiness in Haggai II 10-19." *VT* 39 (1989): 154–68.

Jenkins, Carol L. "Ritual and Resource Flow: The Garifuna 'Dugu.'" *American Ethnologist* 10 (1983): 429–42.

Kessler, John. *The Book of Haggai: Prophecy and Society in Early Persian Yehud*. Leiden: Brill, 2002.

———. "Building the Second Temple: Questions of Time, Text, and History in Haggai 1.1-11." *JSOT* 27 (2002): 243–56.

Meyers, Carol L. *Rediscovering Eve: Ancient Israelite Women in Context*. Oxford: Oxford University Press, 2013.

Meyers, Carol L., and Eric M. Meyers. *Haggai, Zechariah 1–8: A New Translation with Introduction and Commentary*. *AB* 25B. New York: Doubleday, 1987.

O'Brien, Julia M. "On Saying 'No' to a Prophet." In *Prophets and Daniel: A Feminist Companion to the Prophets*. Edited by Athalya Brenner, 206–17. FCB 2/8. Second Series. Sheffield: Sheffield Academic Press, 2001.

———. "Malachi in Recent Research." *CurBS* 3 (1995): 81–94.

Patrick, Frank Y. "Time and Tradition in the Book of Haggai." In *Tradition in Transition: Haggai and Zechariah 1–8 in the Trajectory of Hebrew Theology*. Edited by Mark J. Boda and Michael H. Floyd, 40–55. New York: T&T Clark, 2008.

Petersen, David L. *Haggai and Zechariah 1–8: A Commentary*. Philadelphia: Westminster, 1984.

Power, Nina. "Capitalism, Consumerism, and Feminism." *New Left Project*. 25 February 2010. http://www.newleftproject.org/index.php.site/article_comments/capitalism_consumerism_and_feminism.

Prinsloo, Willem S. "The Cohesion of Haggai 1:4-11." In *"Wünschet Jerusalem Frieden": Collected Communications to the XIIth Congress of the International Organization for the Study of the Old Testament, Jerusalem 1986*. Edited by Matthias Augustin and Klaus-Dietrich Schunck, 337–43. Frankfurt am Main: Peter Lang, 1988.

Redditt, Paul L. *Haggai, Zechariah, Malachi*. Grand Rapids, MI: Eerdmans, 1995.

Reeser, Todd W. *Masculinities in Theory: An Introduction*. West Sussex, UK: Wiley-Blackwell, 2010.

Reinhartz, Adele. "Feminist Criticism and Biblical Studies on the Verge of the Twenty-First Century." In *A Feminist Companion to Reading the Bible: Approaches, Methods and Strategies*. Edited by Athalya Brenner and Carole Fontaine, 30–38. Sheffield: Sheffield Academic, 1997.

Richardson, Riché. *Black Masculinity and the U.S. South: From Uncle Tom to Gangsta*. Athens: University of Georgia, 2007.

Rogland, Max. "Haggai 2, 17: A New Analysis." *Bib* 88 (2007): 553–57.

———. "Text and Temple in Haggai 2, 5." *ZAW* 119 (2007): 410–15.

Rowe, Aimee Carrillo. "Be Longing: Toward a Feminist Politics of Relation." *NWSA Journal* 17 (2005): 15–46.

Scalfari, Eugenion. "The Pope: How the Church Will Change." *La Repubblica*. 1 October 2013. http://www.repubblica.it/cultura/2013/10/01/news/pope_s_conversation_with_scalfari_english-67643118/.

Schüssler-Fiorenza, Elisabeth. *Jesus: Miriam's Child, Sophia's Prophet; Critical Issues in Feminist Christology*. New York: Continuum, 1994.

Segal, Charles. *Interpreting Greek Tragedy: Myth, Poetry, Text*. Ithaca, NY: Cornell University Press, 1986.

Sim, Ronald J. "Notes on Haggai 2:10-21." *JOTT* 5 (1992): 25–36.

Smart, Josephine. "The Global Economy and South China Development in Post–1978 China: Relevance and Limitations of the Flexible Accumulation Approach." *Urban Anthropology* 28 (1999): 407-45.

Spadaro, Antonio. "A Big Heart Open to God." *America* (30 September 2013). http://americamagazine.org/pope-interview.

Sykes, Seth. *Time and Space in Haggai-Zechariah 1–8: A Bakhtinian Analysis of a Prophetic Chronicle*. New York: Peter Lang, 2002.

Tadmor, Hayim. "'The Appointed Time Has Not Yet Arrived': The Historical Background of Haggai 1:2." In *Ki Baruch Hu: Ancient Near Eastern, Biblical, and Judaic Studies in Honor of Baruch A. Levine*. Edited by Robert Chazan, William W. Hallo, and Lawrence H. Schiffman, 401–08. Winona Lake, IN: Eisenbrauns, 1999.

Talley, Heather Laine. "Food Is a Feminist Issue." *The Feminist Wire*. 12 July 2011. http://thefeministwire.com/2011/07/food-is-a-feminist-issue.

Tollington, Janet E. *Tradition and Innovation in Haggai and Zechariah 1–8*. Sheffield: *JSOT*, 1993.

Towner, W. Sibley. "Haggai." In *The Harper Collins Study Bible*. Edited by Harold W. Attridge, 1265–68. Rev. ed. San Francisco: HarperSanFrancisco, 2006.

Tull, Patricia K. "Rhetorical Criticism and Intertextuality." In *To Each Its Own Meaning: An Introduction to Biblical Criticisms and Their Applications*. Edited by Steven L. McKenzie and Stephen R. Haynes, 156–81. Rev. and exp. ed. Louisville, KY: Westminster John Knox, 1999.

Unger, Tim. "Noch einmal: Haggais unreines Volk." *ZAW* 103 (1991): 210–25.
Wendland, Ernst R. "Temple Site or Cemetery? A Question of Perspective." *JOTT* 5 (1992): 37–85.

Malachi Works Cited

Ajah, Miracle. "Tithing in Ugarit and the Pentateuch: Possible Implications for Africa." *Scriptura* 91 (2006): 31–42.

Allison, Dale C., Jr. "Healing in the Wings of His Garment: The Synoptics and Malachi 4.2." In *The Word Leaps the Gap: Essays on Scripture and Theology in Honor of Richard B. Hays*. Edited by J. Ross Wagner, C. Kavin Rowe, and A. Katherine Grieb, 132–46. Grand Rapids, MI: Eerdmans, 2008.

Amador, J. David Hester. "Feminist Biblical Hermeneutics: A Failure of Theoretical Nerve." *JAAR* 66 (1998): 39–57.

Assis, Elie. "Moses, Elijah and the Messianic Hope: A New Reading of Malachi 3,22-24." *ZAW* 123 (2011): 207–20.

Berquist, Jon L. *Judaism in Persia's Shadow: A Social and Historical Approach*. Minneapolis: Fortress, 1995.

Black, Matthew. "The Messenger, the Lord, and the Coming Judgement in the Reception History of Malachi 3." *NTS* 53 (2007): 1–16.

Brown, Francis, S. R. Driver, and Charles A. Briggs. *A Hebrew and English Lexicon of the Old Testament*. Peabody, MA: Hendrickson, 1994.

Brown, T. Cedric. *Show Me the Money: Malachi 3:8-11*. Delivered 5 June 2005. Washington, DC: Greater Mount Calvary Holy Church, 2005. CD-ROM.

Collins, C. John. "The Eucharist as Christian Sacrifice: How Patristic Authors Can Help Us Read the Bible." *WTJ* 66 (2004): 1–23.

Davis, Stacy. "Malachi." *In The Africana Bible: Reading Israel's Scriptures from Africa and the African Diaspora*. Edited by Hugh R. Page Jr., 213–14. Minneapolis: Fortress, 2010.

Dempsey, Carol J. "Micah." In *The Harper Collins Study Bible*. Edited by Harold W. Attridge, 1238–48. Rev. ed. San Francisco: HarperSanFrancisco, 2006.

DeYoung, James B. "The Function of Malachi 3.1 in Matthew 11.10: Kingdom Reality as the Hermeneutic of Jesus." In *The Gospels and the Scriptures of Israel*. Edited by Craig A. Evans and W. Richard Stegner, 66–91. Sheffield: Sheffield Academic Press, 1994.

Donner, Herbert. "Ein Vorschlag zum Verständnis von Maleachi 2, 10–16." In *Von Gott reden: Beiträge zur Theologie und Exegese des Alten Testaments. Festschrift für Siegfried Wanger zum 65. Geburtstag*. Edited by Dieter Vieweger und Ernst-Joachim Waschke, 97–103. Neukirchen-Vluyn: Neukirchener, 1995.

Euripides. "The Bacchae." Translated by William Arrowsmith. In *Euripides V: Electra, The Phoenician Women, The Bacchae*. Edited by David Grene and Richmond Lattimore. Chicago: University of Chicago, 1968.

Fewell, Danna Nolan. "Reading the Bible Ideologically: Feminist Criticism." In *To Each Its Own Meaning: Biblical Criticisms and Their Applications*. Edited by Steven L. McKenzie and Stephen R. Haynes, 268–82. Rev. and exp. ed. Louisville, KY: Westminster John Knox, 1999.

Freedman, David B. "An Unnoted Support for a Variant to the MT of Mal 3:5." *JBL* 98 (1979): 405–6.

Fuller, Russell. "The Blessing of Levi in Dtn 33, Mal 2, and Qumran." In *Konsequente Traditionsgeschichte: Festschrift für Klaus Baltzer zum 65. Geburtstag*. Edited by Rüdiger Bartelmus, Thomas Krüger, and Helmut Utzschneider, 31–44. Göttingen: Vandenhoeck & Ruprecht, 1993.

———. "Text-Critical Problems in Malachi 2:10-16." *JBL* 110 (1991): 47–57.

Geertz, Clifford. *The Interpretation of Cultures*. New York: Basic, 1973.

Glazier-McDonald, Beth. "Intermarriage, Divorce, and the *Bāt-'ēl nēkār*: Insights into Mal 2:10-16." *JBL* 106 (1987): 603–11.

———. "Malachi 2:12: *'ēr wĕ'ōneh* – another look." *JBL* 105 (1986): 295–98.

———. "Mal'ak Habbĕrît: The Messenger of the Covenant in Mal 3:1." *HAR* 11 (1987): 93–104.

Goodacre, Mark. "The Evangelists' Use of the Old Testament and the Synoptic Problem." In *New Studies in the Synoptic Problem, Oxford Conference, April 2008: Essays in Honour of Christopher M. Tuckett*. Edited by P. Foster, A. Gregory, J. S. Kloppenborg, and J. Verheyden, 281–98. Leuven: Peeters, 2011.

Gosse, Bernard. "Abraham, Isaac et Jacob, Moise et Joseu, Elie et Elisee et L'Unification du Corpus Biblique." *EstBib* 58 (2000): 513–26.

Greenstein, Edward L. "Exodus." In *The Harper Collins Study Bible*. Edited by Harold W. Attridge, 83–149. Rev. ed. San Francisco: HarperSanFrancisco, 2006.

Hale, Cynthia. "Debt Freedom and Managing Your Treasure." N.d. *Ray of Hope: Christian Church Transforming Your World*. Power Point presentations. Accessed summer 2011. http://rayofhope.org.

Hayes, Diana L. *Hagar's Daughters: Womanist Ways of Being in the World*. New York: Paulist, 1995.

Himbaza, Innocent. "<<*YHWH Seba'ot* deviant le grand roi>>. Une interpretation de Ml 1,6-14 à la lumière du context perse." *VT* 62 (2012): 357–68.

Hurowitz, Victor Avigdor. "אכל in Malachi 3:11 – Caterpillar." *JBL* 121 (2002): 327–30.

Jakes, Thomas Dexter. *The Great Investment: Balancing Faith, Family, and Finance to Build a Rich Spiritual Life*. New York: Berkley Books, 2000.

Kendzior, Sarah. "The Job Market Recovery That Never Came." *The Chronicle of Higher Education*, 26 September 2014. https://chroniclevitae.com/news/724-the-job-market-recovery-that-never-came.

KillerGibsons, "Why I Make Terrible Decisions, or Poverty Thoughts," 22 October 2013. http://killermartinis.com.kinja.com/why-i-make-terrible-decisions-or-poverty-thoughts-1450123558.

Kim, Peter Suk-Hyun. "Reflections on Malachi 2:17 (1994)." In *Many Voices: Multicultural Responses to the Minor Prophets*. Edited by Alice Ogden Bellis, 80–82. Lanham, MD: University Press of America, 1995.

Koehl-Krebs, Hélène. "L'intertextualité comme method d'investigation du texte biblique: L'exemple de Malachie 3,20." *BN* 121 (2004): 61–76.

Lee, Paul B. "The Arrival Motif of Malachi's Eschatological Figures in the Gospel of Luke." *Journal of Early Christian History* 1 (2011): 189–204.

Malina, Bruce J. *The New Testament World: Insights from Cultural Anthropology*. Rev. ed. Louisville, KY: Westminster John Knox, 1993.

Mani, Anandi, et al. "Poverty Impedes Cognitive Function." *Science* 341 (30 August 2013): 976–80.

McBride, S. Dean, Jr. "Deuteronomy." In *The Harper Collins Study Bible*. Edited by Harold W. Attridge, 255–309. Rev. ed. San Francisco: HarperSanFrancisco, 2006.

McKenzie, Vashti. "Live to Give." *Praycation: With Bishop Vashti Murphy McKenzie* (blog), 23 March 2012, www.vashtimckenzie.blogspot.com/2012_03_01_archive.html.

Meinhold, Arndt. "Gottesungewissheit: Zum Vernhältnis von Form und Inhalt in Mal 1,2-5." *CV* 39 (1997): 128–54.

Moretsi, Lekgetho. "Tithing: An Evaluation of the Biblical Background." *In Die Skriflig* 43 (2009): 397–411.

O'Brien, Julia M. *Challenging Prophetic Metaphor: Theology and Ideology in the Prophets*. Louisville, KY: Westminster John Knox, 2008.

———. "Judah as Wife and Husband: Deconstructing Gender in Malachi." *JBL* 115 (1996): 241–50.

———. "Malachi in Recent Research." *CurBS* 3 (1995): 81-94.

———. "On Saying 'No' to a Prophet." In *Prophets and Daniel: A Feminist Companion to the Prophets*. Edited by Athalya Brenner, 206–17. FCB 2/8. Second Series. Sheffield: Sheffield Academic, 2001.

Petersen, David L. *Zechariah 9–14 and Malachi: A Commentary*. Louisville, KY: Westminster John Knox, 1995.

Premawardhana, Devaka. "Transformational Tithing: Sacrifice and Reciprocity in a Neo-Pentecostal Church." *Nova Religio: The Journal of Alternative and Emergent Religions* 15 (2012): 85–109.

Redditt, Paul L. *Haggai, Zechariah, Malachi*. Grand Rapids, MI: Eerdmans, 1995.

Reeder, Caryn A. "Malachi 3:24 and the Eschatological Restoration of the 'Family.'" *CBQ* 69 (2007): 695–709.

Ruether, Rosemary Radford. "Patriarchy." In *Dictionary of Feminist Theologies*. Edited by Letty M. Russell and J. Shannon Clarkson, 205–6. Louisville, KY: Westminster John Knox, 1996.

Schwarz, Johann Konrad. "Die Kultpolemik im 'Evangelium des Judas.' *Early Christianity* 3 (2012): 59–84.

Scoralick, Ruth. "Priester als ‹‹Boten›› Gottes (Mal 2,7)? Zum Priester-und Propheten-Bild des Zwölfprophetenbuches." In *Die unwiderstehliche Wahrheit: Studien zur alttestamentlichen Prophetie: Festschrift für Arndt Meinhold*. Edited by Rüdiger Lux and Ernst Joachim Waschke, 415–30. Leipzig: Evangelische Verlagsanstalt, 2006.

Shields, Martin A. "Syncretism and Divorce in Malachi 2, 10-16." *ZAW* 111 (1999): 68–86.

Siliézar, Carlos Raúl Sosa. "¿Ofrenda para el templo o economía solidaria? Conflicto de interpretaciones en Malaquías 3:10." *Teologia y cultura* 4 (2007): 125–32.

"Silver Processing." http://www.britannica.com/EBchecked/topic/544891/silver-processing.

Snyman, Fanie. "Malachi 4:4-6 (Heb 3:22-24) as a Point of Convergence in the Old Testament or Hebrew Bible: A Consideration of the Intra- and Intertextual Relationships." *HTS Teologiese Studies/Theological Studies* 68, no. 1 (2012): n.p.

Spears, Dean. "Economic Decision-Making in Poverty Depletes Cognitive Control." Unpublished manuscript, Princeton University, Princeton, NJ (2010). https://www.princeton.edu/chw/events_archive/repository/Spears120110/Spears120110.pdf.

Stokes, Ryan E. "I, Yhwh, Have Not Changed? Reconsidering the Translation of Malachi 3:6; Lamentations 4:1; and Proverbs 24:21–22." *CBQ* 70 (2008): 264–76.

Swanson, Robert N. "Pay Back Time? Tithes and Tithing in Late Medieval England." In *God's Bounty? The Churches and the Natural World*. Edited by Peter Clarke and Tony Claydon, 124–33. Suffolk, UK: Ecclesiastical History Society, 2010.

Titanic. 1997. Dir. James Cameron. Perf. Leonardo DiCaprio, Kate Winslet. Paramount Pictures and Twentieth Century Fox.

Towner, W. Sibley. "Malachi." In *The Harper Collins Study Bible*. Edited by Harold W. Attridge, 1284–88. Rev. ed. San Francisco: HarperSanFrancisco, 2006.

Tull, Patricia K. "Rhetorical Criticism and Intertextuality." In *To Each Its Own Meaning: Biblical Criticisms and Their Applications*. Edited by Steven L.

McKenzie and Stephen R. Haynes, 156-80. Rev. and exp. ed. Louisville, KY: Westminster John Knox, 1999.

Utzschneider, Helmut. "Die Schriftprophetie und die Frage nach dem Ende der Prophetie. Überlegungen anhand von Mal 1,6 – 2,16." *ZAW* 104 (1992): 377–94.

van der Woude, Adam S. "Malachi's Struggle for a Pure Community: Reflections on Malachi 2:10-16." In *Tradition and Re-Interpretation in Jewish and Early Christian Literature: Essays in Honour of Jürgen C. M. Lebram*. Edited by J. W. Van Henten, H. J. De Jonge, P. T. Van Rooden, and J. W. Wesselius, 65–71. Leiden: Brill, 1986.

Viberg, Åke. "Wakening a Sleeping Metaphor: A New Interpretation of Malachi 1.11." *TynBul* 45 (1994): 297–319.

Watts, John D. W. "A Frame for the Book of the Twelve: Hosea 1–3 and Malachi." In *Reading and Hearing the Book of the Twelve*. Edited by James D. Nogalski and Marvin A. Sweeney, 209–17. Atlanta, GA: SBL, 2000.

Weyde, Karl William. *Prophecy and Teaching: Prophetic Authority, Form Problems, and the Use of Traditions in the Book of Malachi*. Berlin: Walter de Gruyter, 2000.

Zehnder, Markus. "A Fresh Look at Malachi II 13–16." *VT* 53 (2003): 251–59.

Index of Scripture References

Index of Subjects

General Editor

Barbara E. Reid, OP, is a Dominican Sister of Grand Rapids, Michigan. She holds a PhD in biblical studies from The Catholic University of America and is vice president and academic dean and professor of New Testament studies at Catholic Theological Union, Chicago. Her most recent publications are *Wisdom's Feast: An Invitation to Feminist Interpretation of the Scriptures* (Eerdmans, 2016) and *Abiding Word: Sunday Reflections on Year A, B, C* (3 vols.; Liturgical Press, 2011, 2012, 2013). She served as president of the Catholic Biblical Association in 2014–2015.

Volume Editor

Carol J. Dempsey, OP, PhD, is professor of theology (biblical studies) at the University of Portland, Oregon. Her primary research interest is in prophetic literature as it relates to the ancient and contemporary world. Her recent publications include *The Bible and Literature* (Orbis Books, 2015) and *Amos, Hosea, Micah, Nahum, Habakkuk, and Zephaniah: A Commentary* (Liturgical Press, 2013) and numerous articles related to prophets, gender studies, ethics, and environmental concerns. She is a member of the Dominican Order of Caldwell, New Jersey.

Author

Stacy Davis (PhD, University of Notre Dame, 2003) is associate professor of religious studies and chair of gender and women's studies at Saint Mary's College, Notre Dame, Idiana. She teaches courses in religious conversion, Jewish and Christian interpretation of the Hebrew Bible, Torah, and Prophets. She has been a feminist since the seventh grade.